Enigma:

The

Phoenician Anthropoid Sarcophagus

Travelling to the past of northern Phoenicia through its
material culture

Bashar Mustafa, Ph.D.

Quietly O Stranger pass by:

                               here sleeps an old man

Cradled with the holy dead in the common silence:

Meleagros: Eukrates' son: who joined in song

Sweetcrying Love with the Muses and smiling Graces.

Him divine Tyre and Gadara's sacred land

Sheltered till manhood: but his old age was nursed by lovely Kos of the Meropes.

                               And now O friend

Shalam if you are a Syrian:

                        if Phoinikian, *Naidos*:

But if Greek, Fare Well!

                               Meleagros

Table of Contents

Table of Illustrations

Preface

The Levant, the home of ancient civilization on the eastern Mediterranean coast, has fascinated historians, linguists, anthropologists, zoologists, and virtually anyone who studies any aspect of the history of our world and its cultures. Nowhere is this more the case than in the region we know as ancient Phoenicia. The history of this region, today principally the country of Syria, is replete with legend and mystery. In this volume, Dr. Mustafa introduces the reader to the epicenter of the region, the ancient city of *Amrīt* and its island neighbor, *Arados*. Beginning with the origin of the various peoples who settled in that coastal city and island neighbor in the Iron Age, he traces the growth of the region and the interaction of its people with those of other civilizations. Dr. Mustafa gives particular attention to the material culture of the inhabitants of the area, with emphasis on death and burial practices, detailing the Phoenician anthropomorphic sarcophagus of the second half of the first millennium BCE and the typology of various types of tombs created by these fascinating people.

Parting from the historical trend, Dr. Mustafa studies these sarcophagi and related material — the funerary culture — from the point of view of an archaeologist and scientist rather than from that of a casual collector or art historian. This small volume provides a treasure trove of material for browsing or stimulating further study for anyone interested in Phoenicia, the people of that civilization, or ancient funerary practices.

Acknowledgments

I gratefully acknowledge all the help received in the research and preparation of this book. For editing, and especially for help in English usage and style, particular thanks is due to DeMar Southard. For their work in providing me information of excavations, I am indebted to the former directors of the Tartus Museum, B. Alkahat and R. Hosh. I would like to acknowledge, in a very special way, the great help of the director of the Department of Antiquities of Tartus, M. Hasan, for his inestimable support and the facilities given for the use of the museum and its laboratory. And finally, I owe much gratitude to my Ph.D. supervisor, Professor Pedro Aguayo de Hoyos, for his constructive criticism during my studies and in post-graduate research in various aspects covered in this work, and also for the time afforded me during long talks in which we shared ideas and viewpoints on this subject as well as other broader issues.

Bashar Mustafa, 2016

Forward

Some three-thousand years ago a mosaic of tribes with nebulous political boundaries inhabited the coast of the region we know today as the country of Syria. Greek colonists, more interested in lucrative business deals than in cultural edification, developed trade with them but made little note of their cultural differences. The area of the ancient world in which we find this diverse collection of cultures, brought into proximity, each with the other by unknown forces of history, the Greeks collectively referred to as *Phoiníke,* which comes down to us as Phoenicia in modern-day parlance. Eventually, as so often happens, a common geography and environment led these "Phoenicians" to develop a common culture throughout this region (*Fig. 1*).

The Greeks referred to the inhabitants of Phoenician cities as "Canaanites," from the Greek *kemən,* an ambiguous name we find used in the second millennium BCE. Historians of the modern age refer to those same people existing in that region during the first millennium BCE as Proto-Phoenician because of the emerging socio-political circumstances that lead them to adapt themselves as a more unified people in reaction to the exigencies of changing political powers.

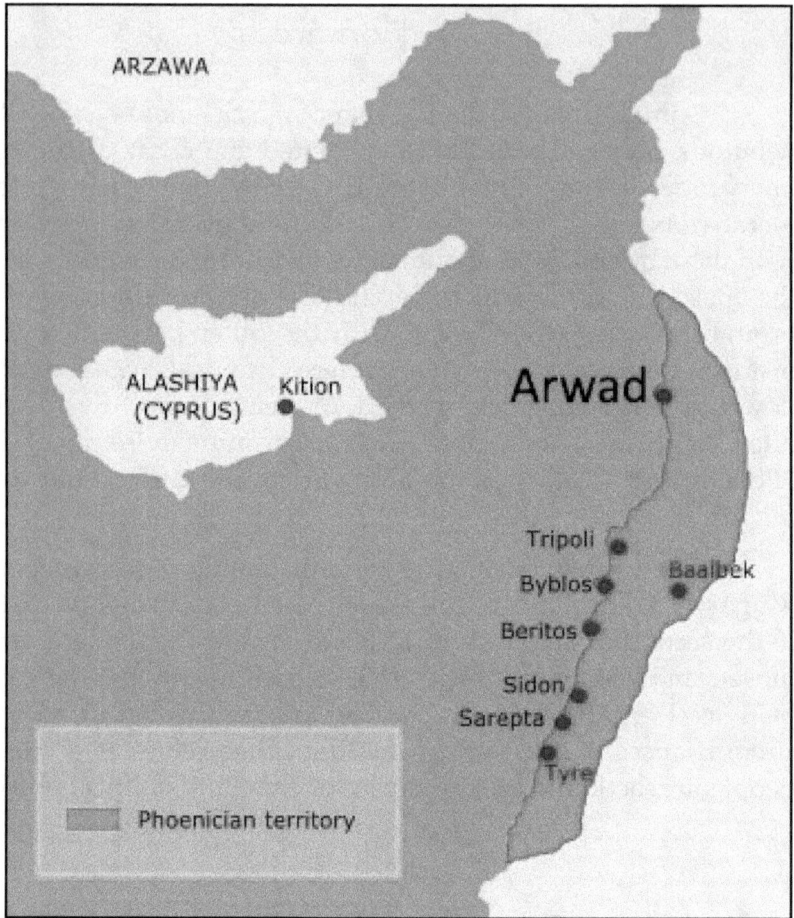

Figure 1 Phoenician territory

But the mystery persists; where did they come from? For an answer, we have several stories with provenance in ancient sources. The ancient Greek writer and geographer Herodotus suggested a Persian origin. He posited that the Phoenicians came from the region near the Red Sea, while Strabo, the Greek geographer, philosopher, and historian (c. 64 BCE – c. 24 CE), theorized their origins were near the Arabian Gulf, the so-called *Gerrha*. He states that the Phoenicians settled this area as a base from which to navigate the northern and southern Mediterranean Sea. He further holds that there were many settlements in this region, one of which was known as *Aradus*. Evidence of a shared culture throughout the region are the temples similar to those that have been documented on the Phoenician coast. Additional information passed to us by Strabo states that on the Gulf of Oman there existed a harbor named Sidon, from which came the main root of the Phoenician culture with other groups coming from the Arabian (Persian) Gulf. To support his thesis, Strabo refers to Homer's *Odyssey* to explain how, for instance, the island of *Aradus* was built by Sidonian tribes[1].

Clearly, the landscape and environment deeply influenced the Phoenician societal structure. Due to the region's narrow rivers and the location of their settlements, on a narrow coastal strip of land and isolated by a mountain chain, the Phoenician people were virtually predestined to live from and for the sea. Indeed, according to Herodotus, their geographical position among splendid forests of cedar on the coast dictated that they were fated for ship building and the maritime trades. Indeed, by the first half millennium BCE, a Phoenician expedition sent by the pharaoh Necao II turned to Africa from the Red Sea and returned three years later through the Strait of Gibraltar. This feat was only duplicated two thousand years later by Portuguese caravels in the time of Columbus.

The Phoenicians establish their territory through the development of a commercial outlet by sea rather than by land. Yet their position in this region, on the land-route between great ancient cultures, left them vulnerable to constant external political and social influences.

The names of the Phoenician cities of the Levant have changed according to fluid political situations in the region. For this reason we must approach carefully the descriptive terms *Phoenician* and *Phoenicia* and attempts to describe the ancient cities and settlements of that area.

———————————————

[1]The name Phoenician conjures a variety of contradictory images — mirrors of an ambiguous past. However, we may suppose they were originally people who inhabited the coastal strip that occupies the current Syrian and Lebanese Mediterranean coast. The lack of written sources from the inhabitants themselves remains among historians and archaeologists cause for strong argument concerning the use the term "Phoenician." Increasingly, it is more common to designate these sailors as *Tyrian, Sidonian*, and *Arvadites*.

Unless we seriously consider the myriad changes that occurred in this region throughout the centuries and give proper weight to the extreme differences among the Phoenician cities themselves, we will misunderstand and misinterpret this fascinating and diverse culture. The history of the Phoenician city-states, especially on and around the Levant coast, changed significantly under their many rulers, starting with the Assyrians and Neo-Babylonians, and continued as they became part of the *Achaemenid* Empire, the last stage of Phoenician culture before its progressive absorption by Hellenist civilization.

Compounding the misunderstandings and misinterpretations of this fascinating people, up to the middle of twentieth century, tracing Phoenician material culture was hampered by the lack of systematic excavation even of important archaeological sites on the Levant coast. Any documentation by the scientific community before the twentieth century was solely reliant on external literary evidence, a situation made worse by the fragmentary survival of the Phoenicians' own written histories and mythologies. Early scholars therefore sought to fill in the gaps in their knowledge through inference from Assyrian, Babylonian, Greek, and Roman records, most of which present an incomplete and biased view of Phoenician societies. The result has been, at best, a blurred and incomplete picture of the culture and history of Phoenician societies.

Thus, the study of any Phoenician settlement is a daunting task. The principle problem facing any scholar or general reader is the lack of accessible, unbiased, up-to-date literature examining Phoenician archaeology. Such literature as does exist is at best scattered in a multitude of sources and inconsistently documented. The purpose of this book, then, is to provide a broad overview of at least a small part of the material culture of this enigmatic, so-called "Phoenician" civilization. We may glean substantial information from the funeral material found in the city state of *Aradus/Amrīt*, located on the Syrian coast, along with that of the northern center of the land of Phoenicia and thus of those people we call Phoenicians. We will survey the present state of archaeological investigation and examine the funerary architecture in the area, with special emphasis on the Phoenician anthropoid sarcophagus. We will examine the majority of the anthropoid sarcophagi unearthed in the area, the greater part of which date to Iron Age III (c. 600 to 300 BCE).

The present book should be considered a work in progress. Indeed, future discoveries, as well as those being made today at current archaeological sites could very well alter conclusions we will draw in this study. Our hope is that this overview, by stimulating interest, debate, and discussion, will contribute to a better appreciation of the mysteries of the ancient society we call Phoenician.

1. The Land of Northern Phoenicia

Before we start our journey, it would behoove us to delve into the origin of Syria's name, to see if by discovering its source and meaning we might better understand this entire region. In fact we find the origin of the name continues to be controversial even among scholars. While it may seem obvious on the surface that Syria is etymologically related to Assyria and proceeds from it, the fact is we find in Greek texts the names Syria and Assyria often being used interchangeably. Another theory regarding the origin of the name Syria is that it originates with the Syriac civilization that started in the second half of the second millennium BCE, following a path similar to that of what is termed the Hellenic civilization. Due to the absence of documental sources or remains of material artefacts which could clear up this ambiguous name, historians find a difficult task in tracing the origins of the name back to a specific geographical area that was occupied by the Syriac culture and may definitively be identified as ancient Syria or Syriac from the time the names first appeared in the archaeological record. What seems clear is that the reconstruction of the etymology of the name Syria would depend heavily on the key factors that comprise the social, political, religious, and cultural milieu of this region at the time of its origin. These factors determine the course of events and give internal cohesion to the history we would term Syriac. This is not to dismiss the possibility that the reconstruction of the name Syria may be related to cultural factors we can't determine, given our present body of knowledge. Indeed, exploring the roots of the name would take an entire volume, but as this is not our purpose here, we'll leave that aside for now.

The current day Syrian coast in the northern coast of the Levant stretches for 137 kilometers along the north-central eastern shore of the Mediterranean Sea. In the southern area is located the ancient city of *Antaradus* (present day city of Tartūs) (Fig. 2). This city seems to have been first established as a service town for the island of Aradus, as will be shown later. The origin of Antaradus dates back to second millennium BCE, but the greatest part of its past remains unknown due to the heavy urbanization and construction suffered by this area, especially in and around the extension of the harbor and urban areas.

We know, however, that the city was taken over by Alexander the Great in 323 BCE and then rebuilt by Constantine in 346 CE, who then renamed the city after himself.

Figure 2 Ancient coast of Antarados settlement

The first Phoenician city mentioned by the ancient Greek Pseudo-Scylax work is the so-called "Triple City" of the Arwadian coastline, the first of which is possibly *Carnus* (present day *Tell Qarnūn*), about four kilometers north of Tartūs and 4.5 kilometers northeast of the island of Arwad. This city was first identified by French archaeologist Ernest Renan[2]. Its Phoenician name, *Qrn*, refers to the foreland protecting the bay of al-Mina and appears on its coinage dating to the Hellenistic period. The parallel Greek monetary legend on the coins reads *KAP*. Undoubtedly, the main purpose of this ancient, small bay was to serve Arwad Island.

---

[2] This French antiquarian was famous for his mission to the Levant coast in the middle of the nineteenth century, instigated by Napoleon III, with the purpose of filling the halls of Parisian museums.

The second set of ruins mentioned by Strabo was *Enhydra* (present day Tell Gamqe), situated opposite the main island of Aradus. Its origin continues to be controversial. Because the Egyptian pharaoh may not have ever reached the northern part of the Syrian coast, we're unsure whether Q-m-q in an inscription of Ramesses III corresponds to Gamqe. We can only hope that future investigation will confirm or dismiss this hypothesis.

About seven kilometers to the south, in the southern part of the coastline area, extends the third ancient city of *Marathus* (from the Greek, ancient K-r-t M-r-t, present day Amrīt). The terrain of Amrīt undulates lightly and its area is quite small — only as wide as a football stadium and as long as three placed end to end. Beneath a blanket of grass shining under the splendid midday sun lie the ruins of an ancient city holding countless secrets of an unknown past. The area of these ancient ruins is shaped as a dual urban layout: insular and peninsular (similar to Tyre, Byblos, and Sidon).

The first archaeological excavation shows that the earliest occupation of the settlement was concentrated in the area of the Acropolis, *c.* 2100 BCE by Amorites, an ancient Semitic-speaking people. This would lead us to suppose that the extension of the deposit was prominent during the first millennium BCE and served as a port for *Aradus* Island. It is worthwhile to highlight the great expansion of the settlement itself during Iron Age II-III (600-300 BCE), which is well-reflected in the material culture of the area.

On the eastern shore of the Mediterranean Sea is situated the only inhabited island, called Arwad (Phoenician *Qrn*, 'rwd, meaning refuge, Greek *Aradus*)[3]. According to Pseudo-Scylax, the distance from

---

[3] Passed down to us from ancient sources are two myths regarding the foundation of Aradus Island. The first legend tells of a young man who set out in a small ship to find his life's purpose. After an absence of some time, his lover started to worry about him. She asked others about his whereabouts and was finally told by one of his friends how sea fairies lured him into a trap and kidnapped him. The lover was incredulous, not wanting to believe this tale and commenced to ask the gods to help her find and return her love. With the passage of a few days, the angels of the sea sent her a falcon with a message saying she would have her man back soon. The women then asked the sea god

the mainland is eighteen stadia or 3,330 meters. Aradus was a small rocky island, only some 1,500 meters in length (Fig. 3). Strabo suggests that it was covered with buildings of great height, each possibly comprising several stories. Despite its small size, history records that the city held sway over the land of Amrīt. Archaeological records give us reason to believe that its position and the fact that it could boast of two ports brought it much notoriety during its cultural apogee. The first port faces to the east, the second to the north. This strategic position for trade routes allowed it to develop diverse cultures via contacts from throughout the region of the Mediterranean Sea[4], enabling it to become the core of city-state power with its own cemetery on the mainland, Amrīt.

The Phoenician history of the emporium island is mostly unknown because until now it has not been systematically excavated. Yet, many historians relate how it was continuously inhabited at least from the third millennium BCE. During the Bronze Age, Aradus was a key stopping point for all ships that navigated the Mediterranean, especially those traveling between Egypt and Ugarit. The Amorite empire extended largely throughout the Levant coast, so the army of Aradus played a significant role in helping the new Egyptian pharaoh defeat the Hittites and gain absolute control over many Syrian and Palestinian cities. However, the situation changed during the period of Iron Age I to II. The city of Aradus had been under a great amount of pressure from the Assyrian king, to whom the city paid a tribute for protection. According to Herodotus, the arrival of Persian rule in the Syrian coast during Iron Age III brought new political organization to the area; Aradus formed part of the fifth satrap that included Syria,

---

to build an island in which she might dwell with her lover, the two of them alone, isolated from the mainland. Suddenly *Aradus* Island appeared. The second saga, a Phoenician legend, relates that *Aradus* Island is the legal daughter of Baal, the god of land, and Yum, the god of sea who were constantly fighting. Aradus fell in love with Yum and they fled together to the sea, where they remain in the middle of the Syrian coast.

[4] Recounted in the book by Marcien Héraclée is an Aradus Island on the Palestine coast between Carmel and Doros. Further south, on the African coast, as Rafina and Araditanusauthos confirm in Christian documents for Gaius Plinius Secundus, there was also an Arados in the south of Crete.

Phoenicia, and Cyprus. We find, for example in the Salamis battle of 480 BCE, its army was normally available to support Persian leaders in attacks against the Greeks. Some centuries later, Macedonian troops reached the area, but Aradus monarchs were still allowed to preserve their political position in return for absolute fealty to Alexander the Great.

Figure 3 Arwad island

We know that in 219 BCE the city of Amrīt was independent of Aradus, but half a century later this relationship changed when the inhabitants of Aradus Island sacked Amrīt. By the time of the first century CE, during the height of the Roman Empire, the influence wielded by the settlement diminished relative to previous centuries. In comparison, during the Byzantine period the city prospered greatly, but by the time of the Crusades in the eleventh and twelfth centuries CE, the region was relegated to virtually nothing more than a quarry for stone blocks used in the construction of large fortifications and monuments for the city of Tartūs. Today this city is known for its large monuments dating back to medieval times. Between 2004 and 2006 proposals were made to designate the archaeological sites of the region as UNESCO World Heritage Sites.

Many scholars refer to the Arwadian coastline, lying between the ancient settlement of Byblos and Amrīt, as "Northern Phoenicia." The archaeologist Muhammed Haykel[5] suggests that the foundation of an actual city-state on the island followed the arrival of a community that fled from Sidon. From that time, uncertain in the archaeological record, the ancient settlement became the base of a new territorial power stretching through the Arvadite territory. Thus agreeing with archaeological records, the area is accepted by archaeologists and historians as the territory of the city-state of Amrīt and its neighboring island, Aradus.

The greater Arvadite territory could also be considered to encompass a larger area—the southern limits being the river to the south known as Nahr el-Kebir or ancient *Eluthere*, and north to the territorial limits of the ancient city of Tripoli (in present day Lebanon). The region would extend to the east where the Ansariyah mountain range rises from the plains, forming a continuous jagged ridge running north to south just inland from the coast (*Fig. 4*). Thus the Arvadite territory encompasses the region on the mainland of the Orontes River Valley, with the ancient city of Antaradus, present day Tartūs, to the north.

According to many scholars, this region may be the epicenter of northern Phoenicia and is composed of these several parts:

The eastern region is formed by mountainous terrain that never drops below 1,000 meters in altitude and separates the coast from the Orontes River Valley. Its plentiful forest areas, easily accessible from the shore, provided the natural resources for the manufacture of ships and other types of water craft, as well as for domestic use. Moreover, the exploitation of mining and quarrying in the mountainous area facilitated the high demands of arts and crafts in the settlement.

---

[5] Haykel was the first Syrian scholar who started working in Aradus/Amrit under the direction of the Syrian Directorate of Antiquities and at the Museum of Damascus, and was Director of Antiquities at the museums of both Tartūs and Latakkia in the second half of twentieth century.

The second area, for all practical purposes reachable only from the south, is formed by high hills and was suitable for agriculture in crops such as olives and other fruit trees and vineyards.

The third zone is composed of low hills that are located in different points of the Arvadite territory, characterized by volcanic terrain, providing a suitable environment for the production of cereals such as wheat and barley, and vegetables adaptable to the soil and climate of the region.

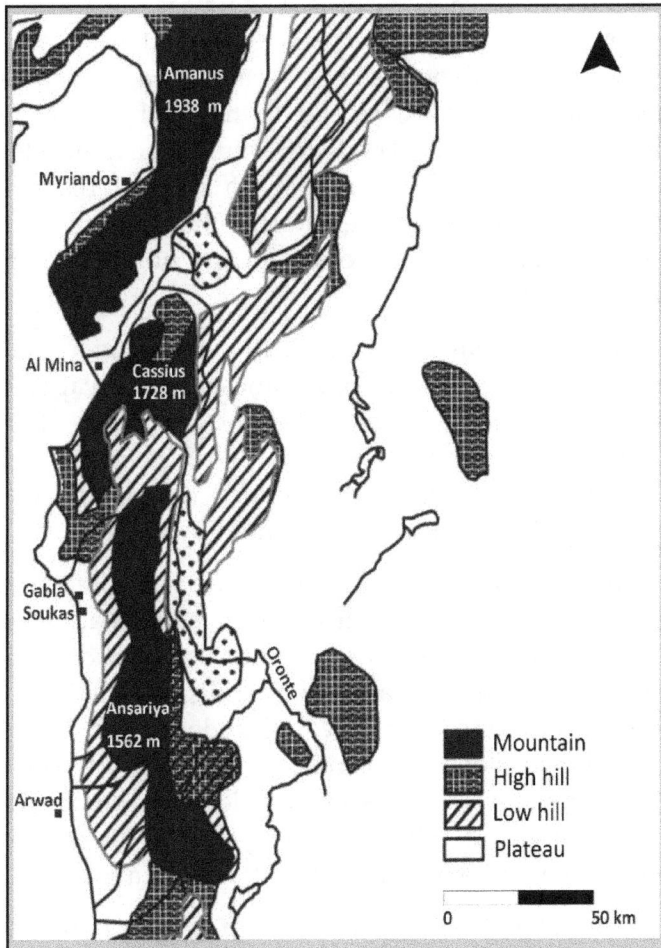

Figure 4 Arwad and northern Phoenicia

Finally, as we approach the hills and mountains from the west we come to the plateaus and plains forming a band that more or less skirts the coast, sometimes penetrating further inland to reach the base of the mountain range itself, parallel to the foot hills. These plains and plateau areas were used for intensive farming and were sometimes irrigated.

13

The water resources supplying the Amrīt settlement would have one of two primary origins. The first is the Amrīt River, running north from the bank of the settlement near a temple and whose source is located about 1500 meters above sea level in the southern foothills of the Ansariyah Mountains. Second, to the south, flows the Quible River, close to a second temple. The latter is further extended by a channel of the Amrīt River, running parallel to it until reaching the sea. In addition, about three kilometers north of the Acropolis we find another river, the Gamqe, with its source in the northern part of the Safita (Ṣāfītā) province hills.

The continual flooding of the rivers over the centuries has significantly changed the area's ancient landscape, today divided generally into several regions. We find along the shore large dunes paralleling the coast, closing the mouth of both rivers and turning them into sand lagoons. Then, further inland, the ground rises in elevation where bare rock is exposed, fragmented by faults.

French archaeologist Ernest Renan was interested in this region in general, and in the Syrian coast in particular. During his initial travels he described the ruins of Amrīt as being of a triangular shape with gentle undulations and small hills, consisting of a wealth of archaeological debris spread over abundant land. The site is bounded on the north by a steep slope and on the south by the bank of the Amrīt Nahr (Amrīt River). The eastern border may be considered the road that links Tartūs and Tripoli, running from north to south through the interior of the mainland at about 1500 meters above sea level.

The ancient settlement of Amrīt and its urban periphery at present are unrecognizable; today the area surrounding the site is completely covered by agricultural activities, military bases, urban housing and business structures, and communication infrastructure, all of which have completely altered the historical area of the ancient settlement of Amrīt.

In comparison with the lack of physical space and absence of agricultural resources and livestock on the island of Arwad, the land of the plain of Amrīt was ideal for farms of all kinds and was essential to providing resources necessary for maritime and other activities of the island. That this area was relatively densely populated is further attested to by the distribution and density of funerary architecture

14

collected in the region, part of the archaeological record compiled since the eighteenth and nineteenth centuries by non-professional travelers and antiquarians who performed predominantly illegal excavations.

Ancient monuments and other archaeological remains have attracted wide attention since the Middle Ages. Today we can see how the city-state composed of Aradus Island and the city of Amrīt has provided to western museums virtually uncountable archaeological artefacts and art pieces due to the illegitimate activities of past travelers, dealers, and aficionados of ancient history. We may also highlight the profound negative consequence of the colonial period suffered by the region. Starting with the Turkish (or so-called Ottoman) Empire to the region's independence from France, uncountable objects have been removed to provide the inventory of private collections or those of museums of other countries. We should note that the foundation of the Archaeological Museum of Istanbul was the beneficiary of looted funeral material (anthropomorphic sarcophagi) that have been unearthed from the Syrian and Lebanese coast in the nineteenth century. Indeed, virtually all archaeological interventions between the middle ages and early nineteenth century were the result of looters who were only interested in the accumulation of artefacts or pieces of art that could be sold on the black market.

By the second half of the nineteenth century Maurice Dunand and Nasib Saliby[6] contributed significant advances to the knowledge of the history of Amrīt. Subsequent to their work, Haykel made significant breakthroughs in the history of both the island of Aradus and the city of Amrīt. From that time forward the directorate of the ancient city of Tartūs took over all archaeological activities at the site, employing the work of local archaeologists and specialized researchers. However, to date only thirty percent of the territory has been excavated. Thus the information provided by the community of scholars is as yet unequal to the importance of the settlement and its remarkable history in the Middle East.

---

[6] Both are French and were deeply interested in the Middle East in general and Syrian ancient cultures in particular. They are prominent archaeologists and well-known for their intervention in many sectors of Amrīt settlement.

2. Recreating a Funeral Landscape

The visitor to the territory of ancient Amrīt views what appears to be a pensive panarama of a windswept wilderness. But beneath his feet lie the secrets of a splendid Phoenician city, complete with streets, houses, wineries, temples, cemeteries, and even a stadium. The weeds and sand cover a closed book of a buried city — a volume waiting to be opened to reveal a past to those historians and archaeologists able to decrypt its symbols and mysteries.

By standards of the modern world, the Phoenician houses, even those of the rich, were modest and humble. In contrast, the tombs were grand and monumental, designed to protect a magic, sacred space and were often adorned and embellished with sculptures of beasts — lions and other regal animals. Their occupants, whose origins speak of a long lineage of ancient cultures such as Assyrian, Persian, and Hittite, spent fortunes on these memorials to themselves, their families, and their culture.

The vast majority of Phoenician ruins remain yet underground, literally awaiting their day in the sun to bring to light the life and times of our remote ancestors. The task is difficult; excavation is slow, laborious, and expensive. Qualified archaeologists are few and scarce. Yet we know the area of our study bears witness to a long history of interwoven cultural interactions throughout the ancient Mediterranean, rich in archaeological sites and related funerary attributes. The people of these cultures left innumerable sophisticated artistic and architectural relics containing a wealth of information about the ethnic and social makeup of their communities and the individuals who settled the ancient Syrian coast.

Phoenician cemeteries were normally isolated from the city by a considerable distance and where feasible, by a natural barrier such as a river or lake. This ensured that both spiritual and physical pollution would be kept separate from the city. Indeed, the inhabitants of island Phoenician settlements such as the cities of Arwad, Cadiz, and Tyre always located their cemeteries on the mainland. Most large Phoenician cities seem to have had multiple burial grounds, a situation that arose for two reasons. First, the expansion of settlements resulted in the necessity of new burial grounds, which were then located farther away from the city limits. The second reason finds its basis in societal differences; wealthier citizens wanted to have their own burial precincts.

The city-state composed of Aradus and Amrīt is well-known in the region for the complexity of Phoenician culture it preserves. One of the best-preserved examples of a Phoenician sanctuary is *Ma'abed* on the Levantine coast. It combines a rich corpus of Cypriote limestone (chalk) votive sculpture with a sacred district characterized by Near Eastern, Egyptian, and Anatolian architectural elements. This site dates back to the sixth to fourth centuries BCE and is dedicated to *Melqart Eshmun* gods. We won't be able to do justice to this area here, for its great importance in history this magnificent temple deserves its own volume of study.

As with all things in all societies, generalizations are inadequate. The people of the Phoenician societies built their tombs in various styles and sizes. However, we can draw a definite distinction between tombs intended for collective burials and those designed for individuals. The fact that this region is among the areas where the use of hypogeal tombs is most concentrated is a primary aspect that makes this settlement exceptional in the Mediterranean basin, and in this respect it is only second behind *Sīdon* (Ṣaydā in present day Lebanon). To date, thirty anthropoid sarcophagi have been documented from this area, providing a vitally important source of information regarding funeral rites during Iron Age III (c. 600-300 BC), or the Persian period. But to accentuate the lack of coordinated research that has been done in this area, the vast majority of cemeteries that contain anthropomorphic sarcophagi in the territory of Amrīt have been unearthed quite accidentally, usually during contemporary construction or road improvement.

Research of funerary architecture in this region, which only began in earnest half a century ago, to date has not provided satisfactory archaeological results. Further, any documentation of the architecture of the graves that contained sarcophagi, or of the funeral containers themselves, has, as a general rule, been very poor and, for the most part, incomplete.

Many travelers have described the funerary architecture of the territory of Aradus/Amrīt at various levels of detail. Coming from an

17

untrained perspective, these descriptions have barely given a serviceable overview at a scholarly archaeological level. The first publication by a professional archaeologist, Ernest Renan, dates back to December 1860. Researchers considered this the starting point for serious investigation connected with the Phoenician presence on the coast of Syria.

In order to view the funerary landscape of this region, let's look at the typology of the many tombs documented in the archaeological record. We'll highlight each one, drawing attention to qualities that make them unique.

I. Hypogeal mausoleum

Built of rock or cut into rock underground to create an excavated tomb chamber, or hypogeum, the hypogeal mausoleum is accessed by a shaft or a stepped, open-air ramp, known as a *dromos*. The excavated hypogea themselves, designed for single or multiple burials, are only occasionally marked by monuments.

II. Pyramidal (*Fig.5*)

The so-called *Maġāzil* tomb (from the Arabic for spindles) is considered one of the most outstanding tower tombs on the Syrian coast, even more so because it is one of the best-preserved examples in the region. This two-tower structure is located to the Southeast of the ancient city of *Ma'abed*, just 500 meters from the coast and about 400 meters from the road that links Tartūs and Trīpoli.

The first tower is *Pyramidal*. Its base is 25x16 meters and is constructed over a circular basement. Also part of the structure is an underground hypogeum, a *dromos*, two burial chambers, and seventeen *loculi*, all topped by a monumental tower eight meters in hight. The second is cylindrical. At 16x8 meters, it is somewhat smaller than the first. It's erected on a rectangular pedestal standing 7.5 meters above the hill. Underneath is an underground hypogeum, a dromos, two burial chambers, six loculi, and a mastaba[7]. It is capped by a huge monument supported by four lions, one at each corner. Sadly, the lions have only been partially preserved.

Maurice Dunand, Nasib Saliby, and their assistants in the mid-twentieth century initiated a formal excavation of these monumental hypogeal tombs. To date, not even one anthropomorphic sarcophagus has been found inside. Nonetheless, many oil lamps, ceramics, and other artefacts have been recovered. The consensus among historians is that this impressive tomb dates back to the fifth century BCE. To be even more precise, this monument may have been built during the period of Persian domination of the Syrian coast since its architecture features the style of that culture. It was, however, in continuous use to the time of the Roman Empire, probably at least until the first century CE.

Figure 5 Recreation of tower tomb from Amrit necropolis

------

[7] A rectangular structure with outward sloping sides.

19

III. Snail Tower at Burğ al-Bazzāqa

Commonly named the "Snail Tower," located in citrus plantations on private land 1.5 kilometers to the southwest of the ruins of Amrīt, lies an impressive tomb built of skillfully-cut ashlar blocks, some of which are five meters in length and two meters high. Built above a rocky base, the monumental tower is composed of two floors, each of which has an entrance in its northern side. The structure is composed of a dromos, main burial chamber, and Loculi. Its interior chamber has a mastaba of dimensions 537x468x172 cm. According to ancient records, this type of structure was originally topped by a pyramid-shaped structure, but this has been lost over the course of the centuries. This tomb is considered to be a contemporary of another monumental tomb in the area of our study, which shows strong Persian affinities.

IV. Cube

Located to the east of Mağāzil, on a platform two meters up a hill, is a tomb formed by a pyramidal shape adorned by Egyptian elements, although only about half of the structure remains to the present day. Cube monument styles have been documented in Sidon and other Phoenician cities throughout the Levant coast. The tomb referenced here is considered by scholars to be a contemporary of the first two tombs mentioned above.

V. Necropolis of Azar

Situated on the southern side of Tartūs city at a distance of about two kilometers to the north of ancient Amrīt, and about 500 meters from the sea is the necropolis of *Azar*. This site was visited several times in 1862 by Ernest Renan, who possibly recognized several ceramic and terracotta boxes of sarcophagi in an area where these objects had previously been neglected. The site of *Azar*, as so many others, was discovered by accident. In 1965 while an employee of the Port of Tartūs was transferring soil to be used in the construction of the harbor, he uncovered the ruins of this ancient city. The huge dimensions of the necropolis, which had been hidden for millennia holding the ancestors of the ancient settlement, astonished the archaeologists who discovered it.

In this necropolis we can distinguish between several styles of burial practice. The first is a simple pit tomb. We find two examples of this style constructed of *ramleh* block. The first was found empty, measuring 226x95x80 cm. The second, 228x136x78 cm, contained a skeleton lying on its back. Visual analysis showed that the person had a curved (deformed) back and died in middle age.

Another common type of burial arrangement we find in this area is the private tomb designed to contain only one sarcophagus, normally of terracotta. In the *Azar* necropolis we have discovered two of these, but measurements were recorded for only one, which is 195x58x30 cm. Each sarcophagus still contained the skeleton. The lid of the first sarcophagus was enclosed by *gypsos*. The cadaver was wearing clothing very similar to that found in Roman sculpture. Even thousands of years later a slight residue of textile remained. Renan confirmed the colors of the textile inside the coffin were yellow and red.

Another hypogeal tomb was partly excavated, revealing its construction to be of small blocks. The earliest documentation of this burial chamber was by N. Saliby. Subsequent to his research, the tomb was excavated by an archaeological team from the Tartūs Antiquity Directorate. The chronological data provided indicate that this site may be from a later stage of the third century CE. The dimensions of the tomb are eight meters in length, four meters wide, and 1.62 meters in height. It is formed by a dromos, the burial chamber itself, loculi, and dome. Many loculi were enclosed by skillfully-cut slabs of limestone. The team documented the finding of a wooden sarcophagus, completely fragmented due to the ravages of time coupled with high humidity. In addition, three terracotta sarcophagi were contained in the tomb with measurements of 105x28x23 cm, 152x35x30 cm, and 192x48x44 cm. In each sarcophagus were conserved bones, ceramic vases, small pots made of crystal, and pendants of bronze and gold leaf. Ancient Greek inscriptions were translated as *Markus* and *Martha*, which may be the names of persons who owned the mausoleum or craftspeople who worked it. At this moment all artifacts documented in the tomb have been deposited in the Damascus Archaeological Museum. Due to the present day circumstances in Syria at the time of this writing, it is impossible to gain access to the museum for further information about these and other pieces.

VI. Mausoleum at Ras al-Shagry (*Fig. 6*)

During the construction of Tishrīn University, a public university in the city of Tartūs (Syria), a Dromos type tomb was found in an area called *Gamqa*, located two kilometers from the coast and about 500 meters north of Al-Bassel Hospital. The Amrīt archaeological site is situated four kilometers from this tomb. On September 14, 2009 during construction work to prepare land for a building of the campus, the tomb was revealed, again, as is so often the case, quite by accident.

The tomb, with overall dimensions of 11x12 meters proved to be a hypogeal complex consisting of burial chambers, *a* dromos, a barrel vault, and loculi, which remained exposed at ground level (*Fig.6*). With the exception of the southern part of the mausoleum, which was excavated into the natural terrain, the entire tomb, including its entry shaft, was carved into the surrounding limestone. In this tomb only one sarcophagus was found:

> Male bearded anthropoid sarcophagus (*Fig. 7*)
> Sarcophagus dimensions: L. 263 cm, W. 72 cm, H. 62 cm
> Material: Basalt
> Period of origin: Late fourth century BCE
> Present location: Archaeological Museum, Tartūs Syria, Inv. No. 3741

Description: The shape of the box is in the form of a human body, Phoenician in style. On the lid is carved in relief the head of a mature male (*Fig.7*), bearded, and covered with a headdress or turban, giving this coffin extraordinary iconographical interest. No trace of pigment was detected on the head or on the rest of the body, which was void of any sculptural representation, clothing, or any other object or symbol.

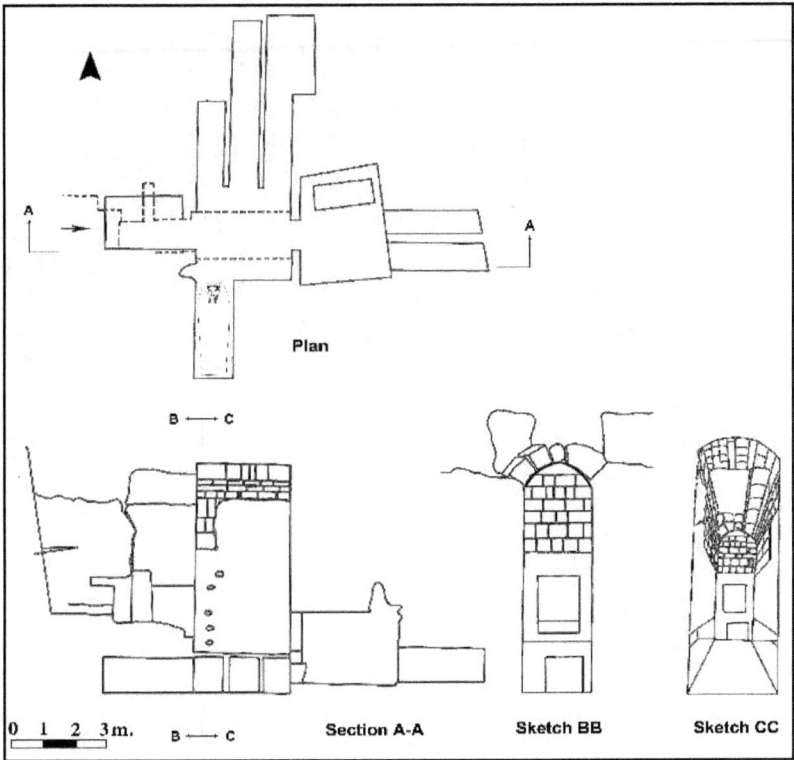

Plan

B — C

0 1 2 3 m.   B — C   Section A-A   Sketch BB   Sketch CC

Figure 6 Details of Ras al-Shagry mausoleum

23

Figure 7 Basalt sarcophagus

Artefacts documented inside the tomb:

Three bright *alabstron* vases (*Fig. 8*) of similar shape: cylindrical body, flat base, a slightly narrower neck, and a slender, circular lip at the mouth. The surfaces are well polished, although in some cases strong calcareous concretions have formed a rough surface. These items are preserved in the Archaeological Museum of Tartūs, Syria. Inv. No. 3852, 3853, 3854.

Figure 8 Alabastron from the Ras al-Shagry tomb

Two leaves of gold. The first has a particular form — a common lanceolate olive leaf. The second is a circular fixture in gold foil with embossed decoration composed of a flower-shaped corolla with sixteen radial petals outlined in low relief converging toward the center. The corolla forms a slight umbo, as a flower bud. Both artefacts are well preserved at the Archaeological Museum of Tartūs. INV. NO.   3855, 3856.

Terracotta lamp. This object has a large pouring hole with a slightly larger discus, a single hole for the wick and shoulder decoration featuring fourteen "eggs" around the discus. Its nozzle is partially preserved. There is no handle. On the body has formed a rough layer of strong calcareous concretions. This item resembles lamps from the Hellenistic Period. Inv. No. 3860.

VII. Chalet

In March, 1996, construction was underway north of Amrīt in a region characterized by high, red sand dunes about 225 meters from the shore. Giant earth-moving machines were displacing hundreds of tons of dirt to prepare the surface for a building project. Fortunately, the machine operator noticed something out of the ordinary and immediately halted work, calling for additional help to further survey the area.

What he had uncovered was a type of hypogeal tomb named by archaeologists who were summoned to survey the find as a *chalet*. The dromos is 3.5x1 meter, the tomb chamber itself is 2.5x1.5 meters, and the ceiling is three meters high. Nine loculi were cut into the walls, five of which contained clay sarcophagi. Each sarcophagus contained a skeleton lying on its back. The other four loculi contained bones and the remains of at least two clay sarcophagi. One of the discoverers reported that a small marble statue was found inside one of the tombs, but it has since been lost, with no other information concerning the artefact having been recorded.

News of the discovery came from two local citizens in collaboration with the driver of the earth-moving machine that uncovered the tomb. Unfortunately, as so often happens, treasure-seekers arrived before news of the discovery could reach proper authorities. Before an archaeological team, led by Mohammad Haykel, arrived on site looters had already removed a large ceramic vessel from the tomb that may have contained precious remains. Police immediately began searching for the perpetrators of the looting and held three persons for questioning. Miraculously, only one day later the stolen ceramic vessel was recovered and the work of extraction and documentation of the tomb began.

Upon opening the tomb, it was left exposed overnight for ventilation due to the condition of the coffins — limp from moisture and easily susceptible to damage from even the slightest movement. The following day, Haykel returned with a truck to transport the coffins. In the bed he formed a layer of loose soil as a form-fitting base on which to place the five coffins. Due to his extreme concern for the fragile coffins, he allowed no one but himself to drive the vehicle to the museum, and so today the five coffins are well-preserved in the museum of Tartūs.

Details of the tomb contents:

1. Female anthropoid sarcophagus (*Fig. 9*)

Sarcophagus dimensions: L. 196 cm, W. 51 cm, H. 60 cm
Material: Terracotta
Period of origin: Early fifth century BCE
Present location: Archaeological Museum, Tartūs Syria, Inv. No. 645

Description: The shape of this sarcophagus represents, in a slightly schematic way, the figure of a recumbent female body. The representation of the head is very elaborate, modelled in clay, and finished with high attention to detail. The figure's face is framed by a *nemes*, which covers the hair. The face is broad and flat with large, protruding eyes, short nose, oversized ears, prominent chin, and sensuous lips slightly curved at the edges. The chest is adorned with a necklace carved as closed lotus flower buds. The coffin has suffered fracturing at the area of the figure's chest, which seems to have been produced post-firing and repaired in a zig-zag pattern. The waist band or belt appears in slight relief.

Figure 9 Head of terracotta sarcophagus

27

2. Female anthropoid sarcophagus
Sarcophagus dimensions: L. 187 cm, W. 50 cm, H. 60 cm
Material: Terracotta
Period of origin: Early fifth century BCE
Present location: Archaeological Museum, Tartūs Syria, Inv. No. 646.

Description: This coffin is also formed by two separable parts, neither of which, unfortunately, are in a well-preserved state; through the ages the box and lid have sustained cracks over their entirety. The lid decoration is sculpted in very low relief, representing the head of a female. The head is large, covered with a mane of long hair falling gracefully, covering much of the ears and flowing in waves over the chest. The top of the head is covered by a veil. The eyes are almond-shaped, the nose is large and straight, and the curved lips outline a gentle smile.

3. Female anthropoid sarcophagus
Sarcophagus dimensions: L. 197 cm, W. 48 cm, H. 38 cm
Material: Terracotta
Period of origin: Early fifth century BCE
Present location: Archaeological Museum, Tartūs Syria, Inv. No. 647

Description: In the cover of this example is carved a representation of a female head. The sarcophagus is not large. The sides angle in gently toward the feet. The coffin has sustained a fracture from ancient times below the waist, with a stitched, zig-zag repair. Above this is a belt in relief, which could be the point of union of a two-piece lid. The head is quite large, covered with delicately carved, curly hair that covers the entire head and shoulders. On her forehead the hair merges with a diadem. The face is round with almond-shaped eyes. Beneath the straight nose are carved delicate lips, contrasting with the strangely oversized ears. A garland adorns the neck.

4. Female anthropoid sarcophagus (*Fig. 10*)
Sarcophagus dimensions: L. 187 cm, W. 42 cm, H. 45 cm
Material: Terracotta

Period of Origin: Early fifth century BCE
Present location: Archaeological Museum, Tartūs Syria, Inv. No. 648.

Description: This piece has obviously been repaired on several occasions. Embossed on the cover is the representation of a recumbent female form. The shoulders are only slightly indicated by the carving, but the head of the figure is well delineated and finished with care and attention. The neck is very short. The hair, with its rows of curls cascading over the ears, falls to the chest. Due to the ravages of time details are difficult to discern, but the hair appears to have been covered by a veil. The forehead is relatively small compared with the rest of the face, which is carved with a broad nose, small mouth, and large, almond-shaped eyes.

Figure 10 Female head of the sarcophagus

5.   Female anthropoid sarcophagus
Sarcophagus dimensions: L. 187 cm, W. 42 cm, H. 45 cm
Material: Terracotta
Period of origin: Early fifth century BCE

Present location: Archaeological Museum, Tartūs Syria, Inv. No. 649.

Description: Unfortunately, this coffin has been severely damaged. As the previous examples, it is constructed of the typical two separable parts, the cover and box. Unlike the other examples, this one is very small. Embossed on the cover is the head of a female. The head is covered by a representation of hair that today might be called "frizzy," although it also has curls that extend to the chest and cover the top of the ears. The almond-shaped eyes are slightly bulging.

VIII. Cist tomb

This simple rectangular pit grave was dug from the earth. At two meters in length, it is perfectly sized to fit human dimensions. The depth of the grave is fifty centimeters. Its walls are protected and supported by four stone slabs placed vertically. In this type of structure the walls also may typically consist of several blocks, precisely placed, one above the other. Commonly this type of tomb was closed by multiple slabs of stone that were supported by the top edges of the walls, although occasionally we find that the grave is closed by a single, large slab.

IX. Necropolis

As is common in other ancient cultures, the Phoenicians made use of necropolises to inter those who had passed from this life. The term necropolis carries with it the very important concept that this space is more than a cemetery; a necropolis (ancient Greek νεκρόπολις) is a relatively large area and thus may be properly considered a "city of the dead," as it was termed in the Greek. Whereas in a cemetery graves are below ground, burial sites of a necropolis may be below ground, but may also be composed of a large number of very elaborate tomb monuments, structures in which are placed the remains of the dead. The *necropolis* of Amrīt was constructed at a considerable distance from the *acropolis* itself (Amrīt) and far away from other funerary structures used by the inhabitants of that city. This leads us to believe that persons of high status — whether financially, politically, or both—who were interred in them may not have been linked to Amrīt. Rather, they were probably more important to the political structure of the greater area of northern Phoenicia. To date, we have found few necropolises near Amrīt itself. Following are descriptions of them.

Bano

In 1996 Mr. Haykel was called when a new coffin was uncovered accidentally in a location he referred to as *Bano*. This ancient settlement is situated seven kilometers south of the city of Tartūs, about three kilometers to the east of the ruins of Amrīt. This isolated tomb was made of simple cist sandstone and contained just one sarcophagus. Unfortunately, the sarcophagus was found looted and full of water at the time of discovery.

Female (?) anthropoid sarcophagus (*Fig. 11*)
Sarcophagus dimensions: L. 210 cm, W. 74 cm, H. 66 cm.
Material: Hard limestone.
Period of origin: Early fifth century BCE.
Present location: Archaeological Museum. Tartūs Syria. Inv. No. 640.

Description: In the lid of the sarcophagus is carved, in a slightly ambiguous, schematically composed manner, the figure that most likely represents an adult female. The head is in high relief, but the shoulders and neck are not well defined. The hair is covered with a veil. The eyebrows and eyes are of medium size and thin. The nose is short and broad, and the mouth is soft, relatively small with narrow lips. In this example we note the absence of any sculptural representation of the rest of the body. Neither is there clothing, nor any other object or symbol carved into the lid.

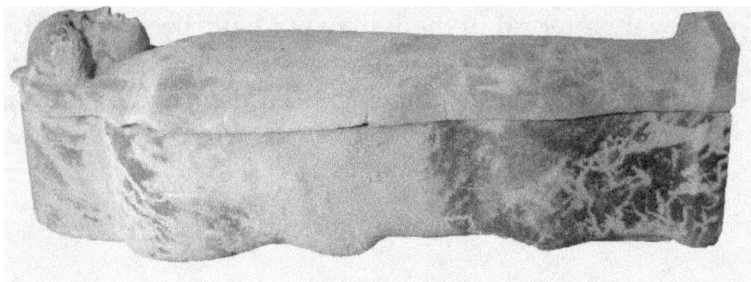

Figure 11 Profile view of coffin

Ram az-Zahab

During construction of military base in 1989 in a neighborhood of Amrīt, the necropolis of Ram az-Zahab was discovered, situated six kilometers south of the city of Tartūs, one kilometer northeast of the Amrīt *Acropolis*, and about twenty meters west of the Tartūs-Homs highway, covering an area of 20x12 meters. The necropolis consists of seven excavated tombs set approximately two meters underground protected by ramleh. Mohammad Haykel was the first to analyze the tombs and found, of the seven, five were oriented north to south, the others northwest to southeast. Inside the tombs he documented four sarcophagi.

1.   Female anthropoid sarcophagus
Sarcophagus Dimensions: L. 210 cm, W. 46 cm, H. 60 cm
Material: Hard limestone
Period of origin: Early fourth century BCE
Present location: Archaeological Museum, Tartūs Syria, Inv. No. 633.

Description: The first sarcophagus consists of two separable parts, as is usual in this type of coffin: box and lid. In the lid is a representation of a female head, carved in relief with high quality and utmost attention to detail. The neck is short and straight, the shoulders are well represented. The hair is long and collected, pulled back from the face, yet still mostly

32

covering the ears. The hair is, in turn, covered by a veil. The eyes are very rounded, the nose is large, and the mouth is small and curved. Noteworthy is the absence of any sculptural representation of the rest of the body, nor is there clothing or any other object or symbol.

2.   Female anthropoid sarcophagus (*Fig. 12*)
Sarcophagus dimensions: L. 227 cm, W. 70 cm, H. 64 cm
Material: Hard limestone
Period of origin: Late fourth century BCE
Present location: Archaeological Museum, Tartūs Syria, Inv. No. 634.

Figure 12 Detail of head of sarcophagus

Description: The carved relief female head and shoulders represented in the lid of this second example has an unusually long neck. The shoulders are well defined, the face is relatively flat and rounded, and the hair is short and covered by a diadem. Her eyes are almond shaped with very thin eyelids. She has a broad nose and carefully carved, delicate lips. Again, the figure stops at the shoulders; there is no sculptural representation of the rest of the body nor any other object or symbol.

3.   Female anthropoid sarcophagus
Sarcophagus dimensions: L. 222 cm, W. 86 cm, H. 77 cm
Material: Hard limestone
Period of origin: Early fourth century BCE
Present location: Archaeological Museum, Tartūs Syria, Inv. No. 635.

Description: In the lid of the third of four sarcophagi is represented, in a somewhat schematic way, the figure of a recumbent female. The face stands out for its symmetrical design, oval and tapering toward the chin. The face is gently framed by curly hair that covers the ears. The hair is shaped in fine, hemispherical curls. The forehead is average in proportion to the rest of the face. The almond-shaped eyes are severely contoured and are wide and expressive. The nose is thin and elongated, which contrasts with the rounded face with its slightly pronounced chin. We note also in this coffin lid the absence of any sculptural representation of the rest of the body, clothing, or any other object or symbol.

Artefacts documented inside the sarcophagus: Curiously, scrap wood was documented upon discovery of the sarcophagus, but it has since disappeared. This, sadly, is an all-too-often occurrence in the history of the discovery of ancient tombs and sarcophagi. There were also found three iron nails contained within the coffin. They are each quite short, only five to six centimeters in length, square in section, well-polished, with heads measuring from 1.2 to 2.4 centimeters in diameter. They are preserved in the Archaeological Museum of Tartūs (with no registration numbers).

4.   Pyramidal sarcophagus
Sarcophagus dimensions: L. 222 cm, W. 86 cm, H. 77 cm
Material: Hard limestone

Period of origin: Early fourth century BCE
Present location: Archaeological Museum, Tartūs Syria, Inv. No. 636.

Description: The fourth sarcophagus in this set is of white marble, especially massive, beautifully proportioned, and skillfully made. It is a work of art in every respect (in the *thecae* style). Different from our other examples, there is no sculptural representation in the lid of a body or any other object or symbol.

Hay al-Hamrat

This necropolis is in a heavily populated area of the city of Tartūs, situated next to the road linking Tartūs and Tripoli, approximately 3,000 meters to the north of the Amrīt site and 700 meters from Tell Gamqe (ancient *Enhydra*). Aradūs Island is directly across the water facing this necropolis.

Two anthropomorphic sarcophagi were unearthed in this area. The first was excavated and documented by Mohammad Haykel in 1988. It was found at a depth of 4.5 meters in a tomb sized for only one coffin. The sarcophagus was found filled with water, but with skeleton still intact, lying on its back with the head turned to the right and arms crossed over the pelvis. No study has been undertaken to ascertain its age.

The second anthropomorphic sarcophagus was discovered in 1999, again accidently, during road improvement. The tombs were found five meters beneath the surface of the road. In these were found five sarcophagi, of which only one was anthropomorphic. The others were simple, rough marble boxes or *teke*.

Six square slabs protected the anthropomorphic sarcophagus of this group. Multiple bodies were interred in the five rectangular-shaped sarcophagi, while only a single corpse was interred inside the anthropomorphic sarcophagus. Unfortunately, we have no information about the body. We are fortunate that a local resident who witnessed the discovery reported the finding to the Department of Antiquities in Tartūs, possibly preventing looting of the site and helping to ensure that it received the documentation it deserves.

1.   Male anthropoid sarcophagus
Sarcophagus dimensions: L. 211 cm, W. 64 cm, H. 48 cm
Material: Hard limestone
Period of origin: Late fourth century BCE
Present location: Archaeological Museum, Tartūs Syria, Inv. No. 632.

Description: Carved in relief on the lid is a very simple design of the head of a male, with physical traits of youth. The shoulders and neck are not well defined. The hair is short and covered with a veil. The almond-shaped eyes are quite large and the forehead consumes a relatively small portion of the face. The nose is broad and the mouth narrow with thick lips. The carving is detailed enough to even represent the area behind the ears under the hair. The sculpture terminates at the hint of the shoulders. There is no representation of a body or other any other object or symbol.

2.   Female anthropoid sarcophagus
Sarcophagus dimensions: L. 213 cm, W. 52 cm, H. 60 cm.
Material: Hard limestone
Period of origin: Early fourth century BCE
Present location: Archaeological Museum, Tartūs Syria, Inv. No. 1921.

Description: Carved in relief on its cover is a representation of a female. The lid is straight and smooth, and tapers towards the squared foot. The carved figure's rounded shoulders are undefined. The head is not too large and is of a round shape (*Fig. 13*). The hair styling consists of eight lines, slightly wavy, covering the ears. The figure has small eyes, a relatively large nose, and a small mouth with thin lips. Again, no body is sculpted in the cover, nor is there any other object or symbolic representation.

Figure 13 Detail of head of limestone sarcophagus

Ard al-Bayada

This site is at Amrīt, eight kilometers south of Tartūs, located alongside the old Tripoli-Lattakia coast road. This site may in fact be part of Abou Afsa. The necropolis encompasses a few square kilometers approximately 2,000 meters north of the site of Amrīt. The road connecting Lattakia to Homs is near the necropolis, and *Amrīt Nahr* separates the necropolis from the acropolis of the Amrīt site. Ard al Bayada was originally noted by Sanlaville[8] in 1970 and was given the name Ard al-Bayada to distinguish it from the other sites at Amrīt. One anthropoid sarcophagus was found within.

---

[8] French pioneer archaeologist who visited many archaeological sites along the Syrian coast.

Female anthropoid sarcophagus (*Fig. 14*)
Sarcophagus dimensions: L. 224 cm, W. 81 cm, H. 68 cm.
Material: Hard limestone.
Period of origin: Early fourth century BCE.
Present location: Archaeological Museum, Tartūs Syria. Inv.
No. 3286.

Description: The adult female figure carved in the lid is represented in a slightly schematic way. The oval face is very symmetrical. The hair is carved in hemispherical bumps and frames the face, covering the ears. The size of the forehead in comparison with the rest of the face is average. The eyes are severely contoured in an almond shape, wide open, and expressive. The nose is thin and elongated. The mouth is relatively small with pursed lips, and the chin is rounded and slightly pronounced, projecting outward. There is no sculptural representation of the rest of the body, clothing, or any other object or symbol.

Figure 14 Side view of the sarcophagus

X. Shaft grave

The tombs belonging to this group are formed by shafts, or tunnels excavated into the rock, ending in niches carved into the side. To date, very few tombs of this style have been documented in the area of our study.

The shaft tomb here is situated northeast of the temple and covered by a dome constructed of small stones. The shaft descends straight down, its smooth walls descending 250 centimeters into solid limestone rock, preserving the same dimensions throughout its extent. At the bottom opens a small chamber where one or more corpses were placed. No clear data have been provided with regard to burial practices (inhumation or cremation). The first tomb of this type was documented in 1951 by Maurice Dunand, discovered when he was digging in the area surrounded the main sanctuary.

Dunand related how the first thirty centimeters was covered by dusty, black soil. Sifting through this revealed bones and various types of ceramics of Cypriote style decorated with red and black linear designs, providing evidence of origin during Bronze Age II (*ca.* 2100-1600 BCE). Sadly, all of the material unearthed inside this tomb has been completely lost.

3. Anthropoid Sarcophagi in Western Museums

In this part we will discuss those sarcophagi whose origins are in the Aradus/Amrīt territory, but were unfortunately unearthed with very poor or in some cases non-existent contextualization. At best, they were brought to light using unsystematic methods of excavation in which only the sarcophagus was deemed important only to the extent that it was a "magnificent piece of art." At worst and all too often, methods of recovery were somewhere between amateurish and criminal.

The science of archaeology requires a rigorous approach. Demanded of the archaeologist and even the serious aficionado is so much more than merely the recovery of the coffin and corpse, but also a meticulous gathering of information such as contextual data and cataloguing of objects found inside or near the coffin in order to open a clear window to these ancient societies. As a rule, the archaeologist must tread carefully because the science consists not of simply unearthing artefacts for the benefit of private collectors, but rather, to exhume remains of past lives meticulously as a type of entomologist or historical detective. We might say that the archaeologist's concern is to open a book that, when read properly, will give us insights into the past—insights that are relevant to present society, and insights that will reveal the ancient society in greater color and detail than previously known and will allow us, in effect, to bring the past back to life so that it might live forever.

From the origins of scientific archaeological research beginning in the eighteenth century and with continuing development to the present day, the methods and conditions of research and record keeping have affected in a very remarkable way the study and analysis of these anthropomorphic sarcophagi of the coast of present day Syria. As we have previously mentioned, all excavations prior to the development of modern archaeological methods were by either grave robbers or antiquities aficionados, actuated by accidental findings. The antiquities collectors seem to be only interested in filling the halls of large museums of the previous colonialist countries of Europe or to fill out collections of private and often unknown antique collectors around the globe. It is a sad fact that most sarcophagi that have been discovered through the ages are presently conserved without context in museums and collections of western countries. Even such rudimentary archaeological information such as where the object was found, its original appearance, its relationship with other containers or tombs in the same area, artefacts that may have been found with it, or other archaeological and architectural considerations is virtually non-existent.

Any scientific investigation of sarcophagi of ancient societies should consider the sarcophagus and its contents as well as the historical context, if such exists, in tandem. We find, though, that roughly half of the sarcophagi discovered in the area of Amrīt are preserved in countries other than those of the Middle East and exist on display absent this vital information and alienated from their ancient sources. In other words, they have been *de-contextualized*, separated from critical data that would allow researchers to glean important information about each coffin and the tomb in which it was found. Absent is the information that might have been contained in and around the tomb that would give the knowledgeable archaeologist or historian vital information about the society and circumstances surrounding the person interred and other information that cannot even be guessed at sans critical detailed records of the discovery. While these early discoveries pave the way to the first publications related to funeral containers, such evidence is obviously not sufficient to create a complete picture of the significance of these artefacts and their implications to ancient societies and their burial practices.

These coffins, sculptures, and artefacts might have revealed a wealth of historical and cultural information had they been documented properly upon recovery. Removal of archaeological matter from grave sites and tombs is deplorable when done by fortune hunters and those who take artefacts for private collections that are never seen again by the public or scientists. Indeed, the disastrous history of looting of Phoenician anthropomorphic sarcophagi is significantly rooted in the volatile economic and commercial environment of this region of the Mediterranean coast and the depredations produced by a romantic ideology.

There is another unfortunate circumstance that exists, hidden in plain sight, as it were, and makes study of these treasures difficult.

This is the removal of artefacts by previous colonial governments or under their purview, with the result that undocumented sarcophagi or pieces of them exist in museums and other venues around the globe. However, from the point of view of some researchers, it cannot be said that possession of antiquities is generally unlawful *per se*. In a sense, many museums may justify their possessions based on the fact that large quantities of ancient objects were stolen from their original locations during the so-called "Grand Tour" or colonial era. Due to the passage of time and poor record keeping, the documentation of their provenance, if it ever existed, has been lost. With no other superior claims, the current holders of these artefacts become, in effect, the default "rightful owners."

So, when no records of ownership exist, what, in fact, defines illicit material? In fact, it is common to find in auctions the indication, "from an old European collection." No documentation of the object's ownership or place of origin exists. Neither is it known whether the auctioned piece was at one time actually illegal. Thus, many scholars consider illegal any material that lacks documentation of its original source.

When an object is virtually ripped from the ground without data, a great amount of information is completely lost forever. The scientific community requires matters of precise context of all findings, as this allows a coherent narrative to be reconstructed about the people who created and sustained the material culture represented by the artefact. Perhaps it is possible, even preferable, to preserve these objects in Western museums until their countries of origin are secure and until their holders are prepared to protect the objects and able to present them to the general public. Schooling, education of the local society, and the cooperation between Western authorities and local archaeologists are highly important factors in bridging the gap of information concerning these pieces.

4. Artistic Interest of Sarcophagi

The rate of discovery of sarcophagi in the ancient territory of Arados/Amrīt has been increasing since documentation of the first discoveries in the eighteenth century. And yet, the process of reconstructing the spatial context of their environment as a whole when found, both micro and macro, remains a difficult task even today. Indeed, it remains an unfortunate fact that the context of many anthropomorphic sarcophagi is completely unknown; we know scarcely more than that they appear within necropolises or mausoleums and in isolated tombs. The findings during recent centuries were beneficial in initializing a scientific approach to these memorial pieces. However, archaeological methods today require and utilize a much more exacting approach. Documentation and contextualization of objects found in earlier times fails even the most rudimentary scientific requirements of modern archaeology. This situation, consequently, has led to the loss of substantial information that would have been of great archaeological interest.

Finding concrete answers to social, political, or cultural questions posed by the artefacts of extant archaeological material culture exclusively from the use of epigraphic and literary texts, the latter almost all mythical in character, is clearly a task that, even for the most knowledgeable, can be extremely difficult. This is not to say that they hold no interest for our purposes, but these texts provide us information in broad brush strokes from a sense of social and cultural meaning. Knowledge of general culture and social mores may lead us in profitable directions as we attempt to "connect the dots," but our purposes as scientists dictate that research is based on documented facts and rigid logical conclusions that can be drawn only from the archaeological material that has been preserved.

Therefore we find it necessary to focus almost exclusively on empirical data to understand and interpret the significance of these magnificent pieces found in the Phoenician Mediterranean insular coastal and inland regions. Indeed, the very fact of the dispersion of findings is an important source of information in considering the changes of funeral burial rituals and incineration practices, changes that appear to have occurred in Phoenician culture under Egyptian,

Assyrian, and Persian influence. This and other empirical data leads us to raise questions that beg answers that may provide insight into these unique coffins.

Modern archaeology places the greatest emphasis on the description, analysis, and interpretation of material culture because this not only *reflects* relationships in socio-political culture, but also plays a fundamental role in the *structuring* of their relationships. Thus archaeologically significant pieces such as sarcophagi, in conjunction with the context of their recovery, may be seen as the embodiment of one facet of culture — funeral behavior within certain social segments — that may allow the researcher insight into how these end-of-life manifestations of status allowed certain elites to transform prestige into authority.

When we analyze these archaeological objects we face a very serious problem: They are normally in a very poor state of conservation, with a high percentage missing the part of the cover containing the sculpted representation of the head. What could explain this curiosity?

Highly likely is that the objects were discovered at some time in the past *in toto*, but the interest of the discoverer at the time was in the object purely as a work of art. This led to fragmentation of the lid so that the portion of interest could be more easily transported to the grave robbers' destinations. This phenomenon seems to have been very common in the nineteenth century. As a demonstration of this, we might highlight some fragmentary sarcophagi located today in the halls of the Louvre Museum. Much of the archaeological inventory in this museum stands as a stark example of the actions of imperial powers during the late colonial phase. Even a cursory overview of the holdings of many European museums would show that France is far from unique in this. In fact, the presence of many Middle Eastern objects of antiquity in western museums is strong evidence of the "cultural leak" of the coast of Syria.

Given the lack of context, as described above, it is not surprising that the corpus of published research articles on Phoenician anthropoid sarcophagi is minimal, and those studies that have been published are incomplete at best. To compound the issue, all discoveries during the nineteenth and twentieth centuries were conserved with virtually no associated materials and artefacts, placing serious obstacles in the path toward full understanding of these sarcophagi from an archaeological perspective. Further, many studies of these objects have been undertaken from the perspective of the item as only a piece of art—a magnificent piece of art, yes, but still lacking the contextual information that would allow the piece to be of so much more value to the study of not only art, but history, culture, science, and other diverse facets of human development. This limited and narrow view of these enigmatic artefacts is wholly inadequate by any standards.

Nevertheless, with the information we presently possess concerning their material culture and with a suitable scientific approach, despite their scarcity we may still propose hypotheses and interpretive archaeological theories of the social and cultural significance of these extraordinary pieces.

5. Material and Workshops

To travelers and visitors of the Levant coast, the abundance of stone in the *Arvadaite* territory was a common sight. Clearly, as a fundamental resource for the creation of elaborate funerary items, this region was rich in natural materials. In the words of E. Renan: *"(…) Le trait lequel Amrīt a d`abord frappé tous les voyageurs, ce sont ses carrières. Ces carrières sont les plus ètendues de la Phénicie, et tout á fait disproportionnées avec la célébrité de Marathus. Leurs contours étranges ont semblé à plusieurs voyageurs présenter des effets voulus, et presque toutes, en effet, paraissent avoir été appropriées aux besoins de la vie. On peut dire en un sens qu´Amrīt n´est qu´une vaste carriéredon ton a utilisé les pans pour construiré des temples, des tombeaux, des théâtre, des maisons…".*[9]

The vast majority of the sarcophagi are crafted of marble. In lesser quantities we also find the use of some very interesting materials such as clay, basalt, sandstone, and rarely, limestone. We know that the marble used for the coffins of this region was sourced exclusively from the Greek islands. Sidon (Lebanon), a city considered more dynamic than Amrīt, was the first epicenter for the use of marble sarcophagi. The Greek cultural hold over this area appears to have been significant, as the large number of sarcophagi that have been discovered here include sculpture in the lids that was obviously influenced by that civilization. Also demonstrating the strength of this influence is the simple fact that the majority of the sarcophagi were crafted of marble from, as already stated, the Greek islands.

The high proportion of sarcophagi crafted of similar marble has led to the suggestion that in fact there was only a single quarry and an exclusive workshop for this material. The output was primarily for the

---

[9] The trait first and primarily noticed by travelers to Amrīt is the quarries. These quarries are the most extensive of Phoenicia, and quite disproportionate with the celebrity of the city [ed. *Amrīt was also known as Marathus*.] Their strange outlines seemed to several travelers to succeed in their intended effects, and almost all seem to have been adapted to the needs of life. In a sense, it may be said that Amrīt is only a vast quarry in which the walls were used to build temples, tombs, theaters, and houses.

benefit of a particular small social group. The similarity of the basic dimensions of marble sarcophagi in our study shows that, indeed, the blocks from which the sarcophagi were produced were most likely from material of uniform dimensions and removed from a common quarry. It seems clear in the case of the extant sarcophagi that marble production may be divided into at least two phases. The first is composed of the oldest samples, which have better quality finishes. The second are composed of a smaller quantity of pieces of lower quality craftsmanship, indicating a degenerative temporal evolution in the quality of production of these pieces.

But we should not assume that the carvings in the sarcophagi tops were all produced in the same workshops or by the same artisans. Belying this notion are the variations in the features of the representations, possibly making strong reference to local workshops. This is particularly the case with northern Phoenician marble sarcophagi, some of which may have been finished in the Arvadiate territory. Moreover, the others may have reached northern Phoenicia from the south, meaning the land of Sidon. The evidence may also suggest that all marble sarcophagi were finished in the Arvadiate territory and possibly the marble sarcophagi found in the current Syrian coast were brought there through normal commercial exchange as gifts or special goods traded among the elite members of society. We can infer this as the result of intense commercial contact within the territories encompassed by this geographical space known as Phoenicia, giving strong indication of cultural or ideological policies and social needs of the families themselves who used these types of funerary pieces.

Pursuing this theory, we may further infer that the workshops that produced the marble pieces, which have only been found in the regions of ancient Sidon and Amrīt, would have provided other marble pieces for colonies in the region of the eastern Mediterranean. Indeed, the theory most defended among scholars posits the production of rough-cut marble pieces was accomplished in shops in large settlements, thence transferred closer to the necropolises of other large settlements where the finishing of these pieces was completed in outdoor work areas. They then became trade items and may even have been used as gifts for the purpose of political gain among the wealthier members of society.

The exact composition of the raw materials, such as clay, basalt, and limestone found in the region of Amrīt was quite unique. In the Chalet tomb, as has been previously noted, there were discovered six terracotta sarcophagi. The use of this material is unusual in and of itself, but the manner in which this material was used to create sarcophagi was also unique compared with terra cotta sarcophagi from other regions. Worth noting also is documentation showing that in Neo-Babylonia the use of terracotta for sarcophagi was reserved for the most powerful among society.

Evidence suggests that there were a small number of workshops or artisans who crafted these coffins. It is even possible that many sarcophagi were crafted by the same hands. We note this specifically in the sculpting of the hair of female images in those sarcophagi found, for the most part, in Arados/Amrīt.

With the evidence at hand, we may also propose that artisans travelled among the colonies of this region to ply their trade. We propose that in the territory of Amrīt there was at least one workshop that distributed its wares throughout the region, even at very long distances from the workshop.

We have already noted that the most commonly-used raw material for sarcophagi was marble, and that terracotta was the material of choice for royalty. We have also uncovered those of limestone and basalt. Limestone appears to have been used as a raw material in *Byblos* (Jubayl, present day Lebanon) and Cyprus, while basalt sarcophagi are more commonly found in Amrīt. In fact, several have been found in that ancient city so it is a natural assumption that quarries for this material should be relatively close. Giving credence to this theory is the fact that the measurements of the pieces are very similar, indicating that the blocks of raw material were originally cut to more or less standard dimensions. These would later be finished in the workshops of Amrīt or on the island of Arados.

The comprehensive measures of basalt sarcophagi leads us to believe there was one exclusive local workshop for those found in burial sites of the territory under study. We also may conclude that it is highly possible that basalt sarcophagi were finished in the same workshops as those of marble, but to definitively answer this question we need more evidence from the excavations in the Arvadaite territory. Thus our interpretation of workshop locations and numbers remains a matter of speculation. Undoubtedly, each sarcophagus was the focus of a specific sculptor who worked with dedication for those who were rulers of, or at least held some political power in, the society where they lived and were buried.

The absence of written references and scarcity of studies in areas such as instruments used, technical methods, and any traces of authorship prevents precise knowledge of the technical characteristics and the organizational aspects of craft production. Yet, analyzing the processes of production and distribution in an effort to establish the existence of local quarries for the blocks used for construction, the raw material used in the sarcophagi under analysis is extremely interesting. We find these gems of artistic craftsmanship serving dual roles, both aesthetic and functional concurrently. Thanks to the employment of artisans in the service of elites—those with political and economic power in Phoenician culture—we have available to us today masterpieces from this society, duly addressed by researchers and scholars of various disciplines as part of the corpus of human artistic genius.

6. Sarcophagi Purpose

In large part, the archaeologist has to also play the role of detective to piece together the archaeological remains of our ancestors. This sleuthing is frequently the only way to open a window into these ancient societies and to try to answer innumerable enigmatic questions, among the most basic of which revolve around why and how a particular coffin was produced.

With regard to the studies of anthropomorphic Phoenician sarcophagi, the standards of research and documentation have not been equal to the archaeological and cultural value of these artefacts. Even though the records are composed of innumerable pages of artistic and stylistic studies covering a large span of time, to date all data have been interpreted from an artistic point of view consistent with the history of art (typical of nineteenth century style and critique), with little analysis of historical or social implication.

Thus the sarcophagi themselves have been treated only as unique pieces of art. Profound attention has been paid to styles and aesthetics of sarcophagi that have been found within our area of study, the eastern Mediterranean basin, with analyses concentrating on comparisons and relationships with other examples of ancient sculpture and architecture of shrines and temples. While these studies have been considered and noted by the scientific community, yet it is the case that the current writing of even trained archaeologists is too often typical of nineteenth-century narrative style, lacking in scientific rigor and substance.

Still common is to consider primarily details of hair treatment, headdresses, or the implementation of the carving of facial features or other characteristics of the anatomy as key elements in trying to establish their production sites or the identity of sculptors. These aspects may be used for setting the time frames of the origin of these sarcophagi, but are not sufficient for understanding the entire context within the history of human existence—the social, religious, political, and economic conditions surrounding their creation, as well as their artistic relevance, which of course we do not ignore. Our thesis, though, is that the purely artistic approach results in more questions than answers.

50

Such answers may be based on the social, political, or cultural significance of the archaeological material culture available to us. No accurate answer has been provided from the use of the epigraphic and literary texts, the latter almost all of mythical character. This is not for their lack of substance, but because they affect the answers in the sense of socio-cultural meanings, influencing the limited archaeological documents that have come down to us through the centuries. As scientists, we believe that research should be based solely on documented facts and archaeological materials.

This brings us to the question: From an archaeological point of view, what was the practical function of these coffins?

The most obvious answer is that they were repositories for the body of a deceased person — male or female, adult or child — prior to mummification. Unfortunately, in the majority of cases of extant examples, somewhere in the course of history the cadaver has been removed from the coffin and has been lost. Further compounding the problem is objects that may have been placed with the body at the time of internment have been stolen or misplaced prior to, during, or after excavation.

Phoenician anthropomorphic sarcophagi were containers of the deceased as an abode for their final voyage, a practice not common before the Phoenician period of the eastern Mediterranean coast. Rather, during most of the first millennium BCE the funerary practice observed in this region was incineration (as we will discuss later), after which the ashes were deposited in jars or urns. We find this even during the period when sarcophagi were beginning to be used to contain the remains of individuals of the social elite.

The top of the anthropomorphic sarcophagus serves greater function than simply providing a cover for the receptacle itself. It has been considered that the decorated top was a way to represent a type of portrait of the individual who was contained within the coffin.[10] In this author's opinion, there is inadequate evidence to support this hypothesis. True, there is frequently a sculpted characterization of

---

[10] E. Kukahn, 1955. *Anthropoide sarkophage in beyrouth und die geschichte dieser sidónischen sarkophagkunst*

human anatomical features, clothing, and cultural supplements. We find especially common a carved head with more or less detailed facial traits. However there is no evidence that these images are specifically characteristic of the interred, or even somehow related to someone else in the same tomb.

We may increase our understanding of the significance of these funerary pieces through an interpretation of the empirical evidence. That this specific type of coffin has been found in quantity only in the Mediterranean basin is in itself an important piece of information. We may also consider the change of funerary ritual practice as indicative of a broader change, most likely of Persian or Egyptian origin, in the whole cultural space considered Phoenicia.

As a rule, the relief on the top of the sarcophagus was produced in workshops according to specific basic iconographic models that were repeated in a more or less stable image type. It has been further hypothesized that there was a certain amount of serial production that enabled a quantity of sarcophagi to be held in stock by the producer. However, we should not apply our modern conception of industrial serial production to ancient times.

We also need to highlight how the phenomenon of the anthropomorphic sarcophagus was nascent in the region of Egypt during the eighteenth kingdom (1567-1320 BCE). The origin of sarcophagi in the region we know as Phoenicia, then, may have been the result of their having been stolen from Egypt during the Persian wars against that kingdom. An alternative explanation is that they may have reached the Levant coast through commercial exchange or as gifts.

Whatever their origin, we can say assuredly that it was far from the land we know as Phoenicia. Nevertheless, the anthropoid sarcophagus would become a hallmark of the monarchy of the Levant coast and an outward symbol to their subjects as an expression of royal power. Such power was imposed by interconnected royal houses throughout the region of small city-states once the direct influence of Egypt had diminished. Other eastern powers arrived in the region to fill the void but were then absorbed by the existing societies and learned to co-exist with local traditions, including funeral customs and, specifically, the custom of burial rather than immolation as a method of disposal of the body.

The variability of representative iconography we find carved in the cover of sarcophagi may be explained very simply as reflective of the variability in the visages of the users themselves. Alternatively, differences may be due to the artistic expressions of the carver. We do not assume that the features carved in the top of a coffin always and only represent the features of the person to be interred, but may also have been inspired by other persons. Variability may also be due to factors such as raw materials, how the stone was treated in early stages of production, and the relative talent and skill of the sculptor in the realization of the image. Further, the finishing of the object may have been influenced by the customer, with the amount of that influence, of course, being dependent upon his relationship with the manufacturer. In any case, approval of a final design would have also been dependent upon cultural norms and policies in the region at the time the sarcophagus was manufactured.

Thus, the elite and royal families in this area of the Levant coast chose the most appropriate styles to preserve their deceased family members. These huge, artfully-crafted sarcophagi served not only to preserve and protect the body, but to provide unmistakable indication of the deceased's position among the upper class of the society in which they had lived. That such a demonstration was indicative of the material culture, and that the acquisition of these coffins gave cause to travel long, arduous distances from disparate settlements and cities in the Mediterranean basin, shows not only the power of the person, but that of the object itself.

While not a true representation of the person interred, the sculptural style of the cover of each coffin may be related to ethnic or cultural factors dictated by the individual contained within it. The sculptural techniques also represent ideas of the sculptor as well as the dynasty that ruled the area during the period of use, and we can say undoubtedly that periods of political stability in the eastern Mediterranean influenced the tendency toward homogenous iconographic models in sarcophagi that have been uncovered.

The lack of documentation in the archaeological record of the period under discussion has deeply inhibited the interpretation of burial rituals in the eastern Mediterranean coast. This is considered by scholars to be a serious archaeological problem. For as we have noted, one of the most important facets of information regarding the anthropomorphic sarcophagus is the context in which it was found that would naturally factor into our interpretation of its socio-political significance. Unfortunately, tracing sarcophagi context remains one of the most difficult tasks for any researcher in this area of the Levant. We can speculate that the significance of an accumulation of multiple sarcophagi in a necropolis indicates the burial site was for royalty or other aristocratic family groups. On the other hand, isolated graves may present us with evidence of a property of a single owner. With that said, we must highlight that both suggestions are no more than mere speculative assumption.

Consequently, the evidence analyzed so far, with regard to the main purpose of the material culture under discussion, demonstrates that we are facing *Koine* in the ancient Mediterranean city-state, where Phoenician influence, expressed by gifts to, or exchanged between parties of the upper class within the various city states serves at the same time to illustrate the variety of ways the concept of power was communicated. Therefore, we may suppose the use of the sarcophagus was a symbol directed toward the living and took on fundamental importance in these city-states or imperial societies.

The continuity of status between the living and those who had passed away was in Phoenician societies, as in most eastern Semitic cultures, a "social union" of both states. This was the case regarding the status of the person, which then extended to his family, through which power was expressed in all spheres of life and continued through hereditary custom and law. Their status was then crystallized and made visible in the construction of ideological or funereal memorials in which were deposited the dead. We note that the very existence and especially the high concentration of sarcophagi in this area near the Mediterranean Sea strongly suggests that in this region this tradition, one of transforming ideology into items of physical luxury, was common.

7. Memory and Anonymity

Despite the absence of literary sources, lack of epigraphic texts, and other archaeological documentation, we may still, using what data is available to us, examine Phoenician funerary beliefs and arrive at some conclusions, however transitory. These ancient people attached great importance to the preservation of memory, especially the fortunate among them—the aristocracy and royalty. The tomb was constructed in order to fulfil the desire of ensuring the person was remembered after death. Necropolises or isolated tombs situated outside an acropolis indicate the importance of the segregation of those burial places from public and private architecture inside their related settlement and the diversity of social life for those who had passed away.

The location of the tombs vis-à-vis the settlements of their occupants' living counterparts was a weighty matter to the societies that created them. Whether they were accessible by a main road close to the city, or in a more remote rural area, they were designed to address a specific audience. The size and form of the mausoleum, the materials from which they were built, and the surrounding protective structures were carefully chosen to deliver a specific message, the most important of which was to preserve and deliver information concerning the person or family commemorated. The inscribed words on funerary monuments were normally viewed as a mnemonic aid for the next generation. Contained in the words were memories—memories of a well-known individual the family wanted to preserve for the future, in death as in life, with the hope that the person's notoriety would pass into the hereafter.

With that said, the most enigmatic aspect of the societies of northern Phoenicia is the almost complete lack of written text connected to the owners of these burial places (mausoleums), related materials interred with the cadaver, and especially in reference to the sarcophagi themselves. Indeed, it is astonishing that these fortunate families, who had the ability to acquire land and materials for the purpose of memory preservation left no images, text, or symbols inside their last place of rest.

55

Given the obvious importance of the preservation of the memory of the deceased, a conclusion that is more than obvious given any of the tombs or sarcophagi from the Arvadiate territory, we can only wonder why the person would be interred without some written record of their identity. How does this square with the notion of preservation of memory? With that in mind, it should also be noted that remembering the dead was not only by inscription of their names, but by offering them commemorative rituals at the funeral such as the offering of food and drink, which oftentimes became a veritable banquet at the tomb. Yet, without an inscription, at a minimum, of the family name to preserve a legacy, the modern observer is literally almost clueless when trying to discover the identity of those for whom these magnificent monuments were created.

We have just a few examples of tower tombs in Amrīt, as we have mentioned before, marked by huge, carved stones that can be seen from long distances. Undoubtedly the family that owned such a monument belonged to the highest stratum of the society — possibly non-Phoenician, probably Persian. On the other end of the social spectrum, most families simply could not afford to have any permanent funerary monument. These less fortunate were condemned to pass into oblivion. Therefore, it seems inexplicable that most necropolises and tombs in Amrīt were constructed virtually absent of any indication of ownership. Or, if there was originally some marking of ownership, almost all signs have completely disappeared. (We will discuss the few exceptions in subsequent sections.) What custom or manner of belief could explain the absence of an inscription or any indication of the person for whom these magnificent and expensive funerary objects were built? From all outward appearances with evidence we have to date, it would seem that only friends and close family would have known the identity of the one entombed, with the result that those with the social status and financial wherewithal to construct elegant edifices eventually came to the same forgotten end as the least among them.

The use of very elaborate tombs and sarcophagi delivers a powerful symbolic message to the individuals who make up each and every stratum of the society. Could it be the case that the memory kept alive by an elaborate tomb — with its concomitant psychological power

56

and social significance—attaches more to the existence of the tomb itself, rather than to a specific person? Can we deduce that elaborate tombs, sarcophagi, and skillfully carved stone sans personal inscriptions were more symbols and means of preserving the current, living social structure than a remembrance of a specific individual? We can only hope that future discoveries, treated in a more methodical manner and maintaining contextual evidence, will provide answers.

8. Funeral Practice

Within the region we know today as Phoenicia, we can categorize funerary practices during Iron Age II-III according to two broad factors. The first is a function of the physical region—the territorial city-state, whether Arados or Sidon, controlled by separate and distinct competing governments with their own rules and regulations. The second factor is the Mediterranean coastal culture itself, distinct from regional boundaries—that homogeneous group of people who shared beliefs and customs that developed over the centuries in a relatively small area.

Phoenicians believed strongly in the afterlife. Better said, they were secure in the knowledge that there is a life after this valley of tears. The evidence tells us that this was the common belief, but only members of the upper class have left us any traces of burial rituals. The cemeteries seem to be underpopulated when considering the size of various settlements. This leads us to ask, where are the missing dead? Some archaeologists assumed that the absence of evidence of burials of the impoverished class indicates that burial was reserved only for the rich and influential class of persons. In other words, a privilege could be made more remarkable in so far as it was exclusive so that the great majority were prohibited from its enjoyment. When the deceased belonged to a prominent family, the manner of his or her burial made a prestigious statement about the family; it demonstrated and maintained the status of the deceased.

Meanwhile, the poor, while not renouncing the afterlife, adapted their beliefs to their economic capacity. The dearth of evidence of humble burials leads us to suspect that bodies of those of the impoverished classes were simply transported to a location, raised high, and either burned or allowed to rot or to be consumed by scavengers and insects, the remains returning to the soil. However, this has to remain pure conjecture as there is no remaining evidence of funeral practices among the less privileged stratum of ancient Phoenician society.

At the site of Amrīt no luxurious marble palaces and houses have been documented. It would seem, then, that the houses of the rich were no better than those of the poor, made of the same humble materials that did not stand the test of time and are today part of the dust of this ancient city. The only surviving structures that truly manifest the social distance between rich and poor are the necropolises — the cities of the dead — and isolated, scattered graves.

For members of the aristocracy the prime goal was to perpetuate the myth of their descendance from an immortal race of leaders in order to protect their status within the society and village. We find the same concept embodied in the so-called "divine right of kings" — privileges that are the provenance of birth, the simple result of being the offspring of an exceptional being. To reinforce and sustain this myth, family members were buried in extravagant, monumental tombs or hypogea.

Thus, funeral practices were, and remain, very important in Mediterranean societies. Looking back thousands of years, we see broad variances in how the dead were treated. Some were buried (inhumation), while others were burned (incineration). The ashes were subsequently buried in small vases. These burial practices mirror the complexity of the society. It has been theorized that inhumations were practiced due to the belief in the resurrection of body, to attempt to preserve the body as it was in life for future use in the after-life. However, the survivors realized that a body placed in a coffin and thus not exposed to the hot, dry desert air soon decayed. Thus mummification, which originated in ancient Egypt, gradually, through cultural activity and exchange, reached the Levant coast.

Alternatively, the practice of cremation involved burning the body atop a large pyre. Upon completion of the process, the bones were collected, ground, and deposited in a funerary urn. This "rite of passage" served to transform and reconfigure the material identity of the deceased. Burning provided a rapid transformation of the body, symbolizing a destruction by fire that purified and purged, giving rise to a new form of existence for the deceased in a new dimension. In the early stages of the adoption of this practice we see a hint of the arrival of the influence of Greek, Hittite, or Anatolian influences, or the arrival of the "Sea People" in the Levant.[11]

---

[11] Sea People are believed to have been a seafaring confederation of

These two methods of treating the body after death suggest to us in the present time the beliefs of the ancients. However, through a simple extrapolation from our own beliefs about the afterlife and experience with the practicalities of everyday life, we may also come to the conclusion that whether the body was buried, entombed, or cremated, the treatment of the body is not necessarily an indication of that culture's beliefs in the afterlife, but may only have been a matter of convenience, expediency, habit, or even, very simply, the only financially viable option for the family.

The relative dearth of evidence of incineration in the region under discussion is surprising. Whether this indicates the practice was rare, or that we simply have not discovered significant evidence to date cannot be known. While in the city-state of Arados/Amrīt no sign of cremation has been documented to date, on a small island near Arados, so-called "Cone" or *Mghrout* in Arabic, writings of various travelers reference human ashes deposited in cists.[12] This can reasonably be interpreted as evidence of cremation practice. In this area there are also tombs dating back to Iron Age III that have been accurately researched to the extent possible, even though the extensive transformation of the landscape over the centuries limits methodical excavation.

In the vast majority of cases the disposition of the deceased was by burial, or inhumation. However, cremation was practiced in Phoenicia and its colonies in the central and western Mediterranean between the ninth and seventh centuries BCE. Inhumation was widely used in the area where Amrīt is located, controlled at that time by the Persian Empire. It is not just the practice of such burial, but the elaborate and astonishing boxes, so-called Phoenician Anthropoid Sarcophagi, that were used that amazes us. Unfortunately, we have very little indication of the treatment of the cadavers inside the sarcophagi. There has been documented the remains of polychrome wood in a marble sarcophagus for a female discovered five thousand

---

groups of people with origin in either western Anatolia or from Southern Europe. They are believed to have sailed the eastern Mediterranean and invaded Anatolia, Canaan, Cyprus, Syria, and Egypt in the closing decades of the Bronze Age.

[12] A small stone coffin-like box or ossuary.

kilometers from the Aravadite territory in *Gadir* (present day Cadiz, Spain).The woman was placed in the sarcophagus dressed in at least four different types of garments—tunics that possibly were represented in the carved figure in the lid of the coffin. The corpse was placed in the coffin between two layers of fine polychrome wood.

9. Beyond Death

The mortuary "landscape" of the Levantine coast gives us insight into the relationship between the living and the dead. We can interpret the state of the remains — the tombs, sarcophagi, mortuaries, necropolises, accoutrements of the bodies, and all manner of related artefacts — and the topographical and geographical separation throughout the territory as indicative of the belief that the region comprised both sacred and secular space. Social beliefs were determined by local ideologies, whether inherited from the past or assuming new meanings through the incorporation of new practices. Further, we may assume that socio-political domination of the eastern Mediterranean coast was integrated with local practices in the city-states of Amrīt.

As true heirs to the ancient faith of the proto-Syrian culture and being tied to Ugaritic and Egyptian myths, it is safe to assume that the Phoenicians conceived of Death as a super natural being. In Ugaritic mythology, death played a prominent role in the early history of the Levant and their known world. The various Phoenician beliefs, as with those of other Near Eastern societies, were organized around the locus of the agricultural life. This affects significantly the ideology of the Phoenician afterlife. Sacrifices were offered in celebration of the New Year, at the beginning of plowing, and during harvest seasons. Central to this cycle in this region was the spring equinox and resurrection of various earth fertility deities such as *Melqart* and *Eshmun*.

Strongly tied to the agricultural social environment, the moon played a significant role in Phoenician culture. The concepts of regeneration and rebirth were usually associated with the moon as it waxed, waned, and then disappeared and reappeared through its lunar cycle. The Phoenicians seem to have believed that the moon died each month and was resurrected by its own efforts to begin the cycle again.

For the Phoenicians, death was tied to ancient anthropological concepts that distinguish within the body two elements: *nephesh* or vegetative soul, and *Rouah* or spiritual soul. In the texts of *Ras Shamra* only *nephesh* appears, sometimes called *Barlat.* According to some historians, the importance of *Rouah* could be a relatively late product of cultural evolution. So while *Rouah* leaves the body after death, the *nephesh* remains, requiring food and water. This then becomes a significant element of the burial ritual.

Ancient society probably felt that death in one world was the beginning of life in another. Consequently they either prepared the dead or buried them in a way that suited the expected afterlife circumstances. This brings us to the mystery of the nature of the experience, according to Phoenician belief, that awaited the deceased after he or she was put in the grave. This question has been raised by many researchers and, although their responses differ, they can be summarized in two points.

One scenario was that the deceased endured an interminable, slow, dull existence. Therefore they were provided in the grave with those essential objects they possessed while alive. We find evidence for this practice in the Phoenician tombs excavated in the Arvadiate territory in which have been found with the deceased everyday items such as pottery, jewelry, and lamps, as well as food and drink. This, then, presupposes the concept of material survival, as these accoutrements represent the provision of items that will aid the deceased in the afterlife. Alternatively, there is evidence that the Phoenicians believed the stay in the tomb was of an unknown duration, after which time the *Rouah* undertook the journey to the city of the dead. The belief in a funeral journey, the need to reach the world of the dead, is attested to in the figure of the funerary boat found on numerous sarcophagi found in the region of the Levant coast.

The body would be placed in the tomb, laid out in a sarcophagus, or more commonly, simply placed on a cut rock. In the case of kings, or particularly affluent or important elite members of society, there are indications that the body would also have been mummified and treated according to Phoenician belief. According to the archaeological record, many bodies were buried in a single tomb, a practice well documented elsewhere in the Near East. It is also likely the closing of a tomb would be accompanied by libation outside the tomb and the burning of incense. In addition, vases, typically of *alabastron*, were left in the tomb. These served to hold the ointments or aromatic oils often used for apotropaic purposes and for ritual cleansing and purifying of the cadaver.

It is impossible to trace, according to Phoenician eschatology, precisely what was believed to occur to an individual after death. But we can speculate there seems to have been made little distinction between the body and the soul. Information gathered from various archaeological excavations indicates the tomb was considered to be the deceased's eternal dwelling.

With reference to eternity in the Phoenician belief system, we cannot avoid one of the most important and long-lived myths, that of the so-called *Sun bird, firebird,* or the better-known *Phoenix.* The origin of this tale may derive from an ancient Egyptian mythological character known as *Bno,* who was described as the Sun God. It had the appearance of a heron, even though the legend relates the sun with the falcon. We should note, however, that while some scholars find the firebird's origins in Egypt, others argue for an Indian origin.

Leaving aside for now the origin of this myth, we turn to the Phoenician firebird. The story tells of a magnificent bird that lived for five hundred years, feeding on aromatic herbs and filling the air with its heavenly song. This bird arrived in the land of Phoenicia where she remained three days. The first day she made a nest of herbs on the Temple of the Sun; the scent of amber from the nest flowing through the air. On the second day, when the sun rose its intense light caused the nest to burn with the Phoenix in it. All that remained was a worm among the ashes. But on the third day, the same sun shone on the worm, giving it wings and transforming it into the Phoenix once again. The great Phoenix then takes wing and leaves for her mother land.

Another myth, *Phoenix dactylifera* or *Phoenician tree* has come down to us from this culture. This tree was considered a holy object for the peoples of the ancient Near East, and was considered the tree of life for the Sumerian culture, from which the myth was imported when people from that culture migrated to the Levant coast. A discovery in the Levant coast of a clay tablet has been documented depicting a small group of men and a separate group of women. Between the two groups stands a *Phoenix dactylifera.* A serpent appears behind the women. Many historians consider this Sumerian myth the origin of the creation story in *Genesis,* the first book of the Jewish *Torah.* This would then be the tree of life or knowledge in Paradise, the Garden of Eden.

The myth of the Babylonian goddess of fertility, *Ishtar*, bears strong resemblance to that of the *Phoenix dactylifera*. For this culture there was a strong relationship between the concept of death and the *Phoenix dactylifera*, both symbolizing rebirth or reincarnation, and as such, eternal life.

So for the Phoenician, the Phoenix bird and the *dactylifera* tree were the main symbols of eternity and everlasting life. These myths were inherited from previous societies and cultures with evidence of their beginning in the most ancient, the Sumerian. Myths are never invented by one person, but through the shared imagination, emotions, and life experiences of an entire people, growing organically from within their midst as generations pass. The mythological mentality itself, then, has its own eternal life, being reborn again and again through successive cultures.

The tomb itself was possibly a place of meeting, perhaps even serving as a venue for family social activities during the day. At night would come the stories built around the burial site from furtive imaginations, demonstrating proof of the fascination of these venerable monuments. That these enigmatic shrines still arouse such interest today bears witness to the power of these manifestations of human artistry, craftsmanship, belief, mythology, and cultural heritage we share even thousands of years later.

Personal objects play a significant role in tombs and the development of funerary rituals. Therefore, the social value of the varied elements of funerary culture constitute critical variables we analyze because they differentiate so strongly one society from another. Further, these factors provide stark contrast between the Phoenician aristocracy—the political and wealthy elite who utilized specialized funerary monuments in Aradus/Amrīt—and the rest of the society in which they lived and died.

The political elite and wealthy families who used very special funerary monuments in the city-state were, in essence, seeking to impress anyone and everyone who might pass along the great arterial roads with the tomb's size, form, and artistic decoration. In this manner they expressed the importance of a "culture of death" as a way to link, with profound significance, the living society with their deceased ancestors on the Mediterranean coast.

The tomb was a physical location where the non-physical dead were thought of as being in some manner present, or where those who had passed could be remembered and their spirits (*manes*) honored. The use of the anthropomorphic sarcophagus was considered a marker of prosperity, but at the same time it was an expression of a new belief, a cult as it were, where the idea of the destruction of the body of a loved one by fire had become unbearable. To be protected within a timeless sarcophagus within a fortified tomb could represent the idea that the deceased would exist into eternity and thereby be remembered forever. Such an attitude and the astonishing degree to which each tomb was internalized and sentimentalized indicates the extent to which these ancient societies desired to commemorate their ancestors for eternity.

Appendix

The word sarcophagus was used by *Plinius* to mean a special kind of stone. In the Greek, from σαρκοφαγός, the word literally means "flesh eating" and was typically used with funerary connotations. In general, the sarcophagi we have examined here are formed by two pieces: the box itself and a separate lid. When the top is carved with human features we term the sarcophagus "anthropoid." Herein we list and describe a number of sarcophagi that have been unearthed in the region of study, ancient Phoenicia, and accompanying artefacts where appropriate.

Female (?) anthropoid sarcophagus (*Fig. 15*)

Originating from the harbor of *Antarados* (Tartūs), which is located toward the north of *Aradus* Island, this sarcophagus was unearthed in 1988. This discovery was made possible due to a heavy storm that hit the coast of Syria; the resulting erosion revealed part of the sarcophagus. Mohammad Hijazi was responsible for its extraction and transportation[13].

Sarcophagus dimensions: L. 73 cm, W. 63 cm, H. 44 cm.
Material: Hard limestone
Period of origin: Early fourth century BCE
Present location: Archaeological Museum, Tartūs, Syria, Inv. No.   266

Description: Only a portion of the lid containing the relief carving of the head was found. The face was severely damaged; accurate description is not possible. Whether it was the face of a male of female cannot be determined.

---

[13]Former Syrian colonial, who was an aficionado of marine archaeology. We are grateful for his greatest contribution (translated from the Arabic) *From Here Civilization Began: Ports, Harbours, and Marinas On the Ancient Coast of Syrian Arabic Country*. In this volume he documented most of the ancient harbours throughout the Syrian coast during the second half of the twentieth century.

Figure 15 Head of damaged sarcophagus

Female anthropoid sarcophagus

Sarcophagus dimensions: L. 35 cm, W. 40 cm, H. 46 cm.
Material: Hard limestone
Period of origin: Early fourth century BCE. Discovered in 1852
Present location: Louvre Museum, Paris, France, Inv. No. 4810

Description: This partially preserved portion of the cover depicts a female figure. Her hair is long, the face is round. Even though the eyes are badly damaged we can tell they were rather large compared with the rest of the face. The nose is fine and the lips are gently curved. The sculptor avoided the difficulty of the human ear by covering them with hair.

Female anthropoid sarcophagus
Sarcophagus dimensions: L. 72 cm, W. 66 cm, H. 67 cm.
Material: Hard limestone
Period of origin: Late fourth century BCE, discovered in 1882 by N. Mitri
Present location: Louvre Museum, Paris France, Inv. No.   1031.

Description: Only part of the lid is preserved. Carved in relief on the lid is the representation of a female. The face and neck are represented in high relief. The hair is long, parted in the middle, and falls in large waves over the shoulders to the figure's chest. The hair completely covers the ears. The eyes are almond shaped, the nose is long, and the lips are carved in a manner that suggests softness. (A real feat indeed for one who carves in stone!) Even after all these centuries, the figure retains traces of polychrome, most significantly in the hair.

Male anthropoid sarcophagus
Sarcophagus dimensions: L. 207 cm, W. 66 cm, H. 94 cm.
Material: Hard limestone
Period of origin: Early fourth century BCE. Discovered in 1888 by E. Guillaume-Rey.
Present location: Louvre Museum, Paris, France, Inv. No. 4967

Description: Into the lid of this two-part sarcophagus is carved in relief the representation of the head of a male. A distinguishing feature of this cover is that it is very slightly curved. The head is large and in bold relief. The neck and shoulders are not well defined, although the shoulders, in somewhat enhanced contour, reach the height of the nose. The face is oval and the ears are uncharacteristically low on the side of the head. They are not intricately carved. In fact, the inside of the ear is filled, left incomplete. The eyes are relatively large for the face. The nose is wide and the mouth appears soft. The piece as a whole still retains traces of polychrome covering the surface of the box and cover. Noteworthy is the absence of any sculptural representation of the rest of the body or clothing, nor is there any other object or symbol carved in the lid.

Male anthropoid sarcophagus
Sarcophagus dimensions: L. 94 cm, W. 72 cm, H. 33 cm.
Material: Hard limestone
Period of origin: Early fourth century BCE. Discovered in 1887 by M. Amic d´Alexandrie
Present location: Louvre Museum, Paris, France. Inv. No. 1574

Description: Only the lid of this sarcophagus was recovered. Carved in relief on it is a representation of the head of a recumbent male. Again, the contour of the shoulders rises to the level of the nose. The head is large and rounded. The hair, carved in large tufts, is brushed with a slight gap in the middle of the forehead and mostly covers the ears. The face, too, is mostly covered by a beard. The eyes are narrow and almond-shaped with large upper eyelids covering the outer ends of the lower eyelids, forming a continuous curved line. The nose is large, while the mouth is thin, narrow, and very smooth.

Female anthropoid sarcophagus
Sarcophagus dimensions: L. 221 cm, W. 67 cm, H. 35 cm.
Material: Basalt
Period of origin: Early fourth century BCE. Discovered in 1861 by E. Renan
Present location: Louvre Museum, Paris, France, Inv. No. 4971

Description: Only the lower half of the flat lid has been preserved, while the upper is severely scratched. Represented in carved relief is the head of a female, which has sustained damage up to the chin. The face is round. The head is covered by a veil, extending below a hairstyle formed by two strands spread from the center of the forehead as if by a central line. The forehead is very narrow. The eyes are small and almond shaped, very well designed and skillfully carved, even with marked pupils. The nose is long and narrow, the mouth small and well delineated with strong lips.

Female anthropoid sarcophagus
Sarcophagus dimensions: L. 39.5 cm, W. 22.5 cm, H. 36.5. cm.
Material: Terracotta
Period of origin: Fifth century BCE. Discovered in 1878
Present location: Louvre Museum, Paris, France, Inv. No. 1293

Description: Only the lid, with a female figure carved in relief, has been preserved. The forehead is rather broad. Her expression is fixed by protruding eyes with thick lids and thin, peaked brows. The nose is long and straight. Below the prominent cheekbones, the cheeks themselves are hollow and flow into the small mouth, the upper lip of which nearly touches the nose. The figure is wearing a diadem or veil, revealing three rows of helicoid curls on her forehead, two ringlets at the ears, and long wavy locks down to the shoulders. Each ear is decorated with a large earring in the lobe as well as three rings in the pinna. The remains of a necklace of round beads can be seen round her neck.

Male anthropoid sarcophagus
Sarcophagus dimensions: L. 70 cm, W. 68 cm, H. 41 cm.
Material: Hard limestone
Period of origin: Early fourth century BCE. Discovered in 1882 by N. Mitri
Present location: Louvre Museum, Paris, France, Inv. No. 1119

Description: Only a fragment of the lid with the relief carving of the representation of a middle-aged male head and shoulders is preserved. The hair is carved in large, sketchy locks as a "helmet" covering the ears. The forehead is very narrow; most of it is covered by the hair. The nose is wide and short, the eyes are small and almond shaped. The mouth is narrow with very sharp and full lips. The chin and lower part of the face are covered by a thick, voluminous beard, treated in the same manner as the hair. The figure has narrow shoulders.

Male anthropoid sarcophagus
Sarcophagus dimensions: L. 76 cm, W. 74 cm, H. 71 cm.
Material: Hard limestone
Period of origin: Late fourth century BCE. Discovered in 1882 by N. Mitri
Present location: Louvre Museum, Paris, France, Inv. No.1030

Description: Only the upper portion of the cover has been preserved. The representation of a male head is carved in relief. The lid has a flat surface with a pronounced step at the base where the head is carved. Close examination reveals that it was most likely retouched after finishing. The head, as the neck, stands proud of the flat bottom. The hair, in large wavy locks, falls to the side of the head, covering the ears completely. The forehead is narrow, the eyes small, and the nose broad. The mouth is small and slightly open with small and narrow, well-delineated lips. On the coffin lid are remains of a reddish polychrome finish.

Female anthropoid sarcophagus
Sarcophagus dimensions: L. 210 cm, W. 60 cm, H. 70 cm.
Material: Hard limestone
Period of origin: Early fourth century BCE. Discovered in 1852 by A. Longpérier
Present location: Louvre Museum, Paris, France, Inv. No. 4801

Description: This coffin was found complete—both box and lid. Skillfully carved in relief on the lid is the head of a recumbent female. The large head has sharp features. The hair is styled in three rows of hemispherical curls arranged in semicircles, falling to the chest in two long, wavy locks that spring from behind the ears. The face is wide with large, almond-shaped eyes. The nose is rather large, as are the ears, the insides of which are delicately carved hollow and open. The lips are narrow and straight. On the remainder of the top one notes the absence of any sculptural representation of the rest of the body, clothing, or any other object or symbol.

Female (?) anthropoid sarcophagus
Sarcophagus dimensions: L. 230 cm, W. 86 cm, H. 79 cm.
Material: Hard limestone
Period of origin: Early fourth century BCE. Discovered in 1953
Present location: Copenhagen, Denmark, Inv. No.   13431

Description: The carving in the lid represents, in a slightly "schematic" way, the figure of a female. The face stands out for its symmetrical design, with an oval face, tapering toward the chin. The very elongated elliptical face is framed in the upper half by hair combed into four lines of hemispherical, bulging curls, arranged in alternating lines, descending over the ears. The forehead is high and clear. The almond-shaped eyes markedly contoured, wide open, and expressive. The wide, elongated nose has been slightly damaged. The chin is very pronounced and projects outward. In the lid there is no sculptural representation of the rest of the body, clothing, or any other object or symbol.

Female anthropoid sarcophagus
Sarcophagus dimensions: L. 203 cm, W. 45 cm, H. 90 cm.
Material: Hard limestone
Period of origin: Late fourth century BCE
Present location: Archaeological Museum, Istanbul, Turkey, Inv. No. 791

Description: In this example the sarcophagus itself is carved in the shape of a human figure. The head of an adult female is sculpted in very bold relief. Overall, the face is oval, but with a pointed chin and pronounced cheeks. The head is small, but prominent with gently undulating hair, retaining traces of polychrome, carved in delicate strands forming a kind of turban covering the ears. The eyes are small and slightly almond shaped. The nose, straight and narrow, sits above a small mouth. No other part of the body is sculpted in the lid, nor is there any type of clothing or other object or symbol.

Female anthropoid sarcophagus
Sarcophagus dimensions: L. 206 cm, W. 53 cm, H. 75 cm.
Material: Basalt
Period of origin: Early fourth century BCE
Present location: Archaeological Museum, Istanbul, Turkey, Inv. No. 1414.

Description: Carved in relief on the lid of this sarcophagus is the head of what appears to be a female figure. The face has been damaged at the height of the mouth and nose. The face is oval and the head is covered almost entirely by a type of headdress, appearing to be a turban, twisting and finishing in a spiral below the schematic line. The ears are quite large, while the mouth is small, giving the appearance of a certain coarseness in the carving. The neck and shoulders are not well defined. Of note is the presence at the top of the sculpture of superimposed hands on the chest grasping a rod. The rod extends the length of the lid and is crowned with the head of an animal, appearing most likely to be that of a horse.

Female anthropoid sarcophagus
Sarcophagus dimensions: L. 293 cm, W. 44 cm, H. 66 cm.
Material: Hard limestone
Period of origin: Late fourth century BCE
Present location: Archaeological Museum, Istanbul, Turkey, Inv. No. 792

Description: The sarcophagus is carved to represent an adult female. The shoulders and shoulder girdle are prominent and very clearly defined. The head is sculpted in high relief with a narrow, elongated face. The hair is sculpted in thin waves with slight sideways movements, covering the ears. The head is covered by a veil. The eyes are small and are skillfully carved to include eyelids. The chin is slightly curved. The mouth is small with curved lips. Noteworthy is the absence of any sculptural representation of the rest of the body. Nor is there clothing or any other objects. The box is very deep and has a vertical break at shoulder height. At the top of the foot of the sarcophagus is inscribed the Greek letter Δ.

Female anthropoid sarcophagus
Sarcophagus dimensions: L. 68 cm, W. 52 cm, H. 32 cm.
Material: Basalt
Period of origin: Early fourth century BCE, discovered by G. Mendel
Present location: Archaeological Museum, Istanbul, Turkey, Inv. No. 1884

Description: The only part of this coffin that has been preserved is the carved female head. It is large, with a broad face, with the hair carved as an entire unit—no strands or groups of strands have been represented. The eyes are large and sunken, the forehead is broad, but the nose and mouth are small in comparison.

Female anthropoid sarcophagus
Sarcophagus (partial lid) dimension: L. 90 cm, W. 73 cm.
Material: Basalt
Period of origin: Early fourth century BCE
Present location: Archaeological Museum, Beirut, Lebanon. This item has no registry number.

Description: Only the top of the lid has been preserved, into which is sculpted the representation of a female head with a short neck. The face is round. The hair is sculpted in long, flowing, wavy locks of combed ripples covering the ears and falling to the chest. The figure has a broad forehead and a small mouth, with the lower lip notably thicker than the upper. The nose is short and in poor condition. The eyes are small and close together and, oddly, the left is slightly larger than the right. A rim resembling a veil frames the head. There is a line at the base of the neck, possibly representing a tunic or dress.

Male anthropoid sarcophagus
Sarcophagus dimensions: L. 76 cm, W. 82 cm, H. 39 cm.
Material: Hard limestone
Period of origin: Late fourth century BCE
Present location: Archaeological Museum, Basel, Switzerland, Inv. No. 249

Description: The only part of this coffin that remains is a part of the lid with the sculpted representation of the head and shoulder of a young individual, probably male. Even given the poor condition of the remains, one can still easily see that the neck was intricately carved. The face of this individual is oval. The forehead, cheekbones, and hair are covered by a veil or cap, from which peeks short hair in wavy locks, spreading from the center of the forehead. The mouth is small with uneven lips, the lower thicker than the top. The nose is long, straight, and narrow. The large, rounded eyes seem very open and are accentuated by the eyebrows and eyelids lined with thick lines.

Male anthropoid sarcophagus
Sarcophagus dimensions: L. 46 cm, W. 40 cm, H. 26 cm.
Material: Hard limestone
Period of origin: Early fourth century BCE
Present location: Archaeological Museum, Basel, Switzerland, Inv. No. 250.

Description: Only the head of this piece has been conserved. It is skillfully carved, although the sex of the figure is not determinable with certainty; most likely it is a juvenile male. The face is oval, with a high forehead and full cheeks. The short, wavy hair is arranged in horizontal sections that open on both sides of the face and cover half of the large ears. From the middle, the forehead is covered by a veil. The figure has a small mouth with thick lips, the lower of which protrudes significantly. The nose is long, straight, and slightly wider than might be expected. The eyes, with curved, thin eyelids are very large and round, serving to somewhat obscure the eyelashes and eyebrows.

Male anthropoid sarcophagus
Sarcophagus dimensions: no data available
Material: Hard limestone
Period of origin: Late fourth century BCE
Present location: Archaeological Museum, Hildesheim, Germany, Inv. No. 1775.

Description: Only the upper part of the lid of this sarcophagus has been conserved, on which is carved in relief the representation of the head of a recumbent female. The figure's face is oval, with full cheeks and a narrow forehead. The thick hair is combed in undulating strands arranged from the center of the forehead. The rest of the head is covered by a veil. The chin is small and slightly protruding. The mouth is also small but with very thick lips. The nose is wide, straight, and short. Surprisingly, the surface of the coffin is worn very little.

Artefacts

1. Gold earring, Length: 3.7 cm, weight: 7.2 grams. Present location: Oxford, England, Ashmolean Museum, Bomford Collection (Previously located in Paris as part of the Clercq Collection) Inv. No. (658, 659).

2. Five gold rings. Present location: Paris, France. Inv. No. (1285, 1286).

    a. Ring 1: Length: 4.9 cm, width 3.3 cm, weight 27 grams

    b. Ring 2: Length. 2 cm, width: 2.25 cm, weight: 7.5 gram. Inv. No. 2128

c. Ring 3: Length: 2.45 cm, width: 1.65 cm, weight: 28 grams. Inv. No. 2086

d. Ring 4: Length: 1.6 cm, width 1.7 cm, weight: 3.5 gram. Inv. No. 2790

e. Ring 5: (no dimensions available) Inv. No. 2785.

3. Ring with a standing female figure in gold. Length: 1.5 cm, width: 1.7 cm, weight: 3 grams. Present location: Paris, France. INV. NO. 2828.

4. Ring with a gold lion figure. Length: 1.5 cm, width 1.8 cm, weight: 3 grams. Present location: Paris, France. INV. NO. 2870.

5. Gold amulet. Length: 1.4 cm, width: 0.5 cm, weight: 6.7 grams. Present location: Paris, France. INV. NO. 1418.

Index

Glossary

acropolis
: The upper fortified part of an ancient city.

alabastron:
: A perfume or ointment jar with a flattened lip and narrow mouth and an elongated body rounded at the bottom.

Amorite Empire:
: These were people of an ancient Semitic-speaking civilization, from ancient Syria, occupied large parts of southern Mesopotamia from the twenty-first century BCE to the end of the seventeenth century BCE

Eshmun:
: Phoenician god of healing.

gypsos:
: A soft sulphate mineral, was used in antiquity to enclose many sarcophagi in Phoenicia, especially those made of terracotta, in order to protect the deceased.

Herodotus:
: Greek historian who lived in the fifth century BCE (c. 484–425 BCE). Widely referred to as "The Father of History."

Iron Age:
: The period characterized by the development and use of iron in weaponry and the effects of daily use. Iron Age I in the area under study here, the Levantine coast of present day Syria, is generally noted as from roughly 2100 to 1800 BCE, Iron Age II from around 1800 to 1060 BCE, and Iron Age III from 1060 to 200 BCE.

Koine
: From Greek (κοινὴ διάλεκτος), the common dialect, also known as Alexandrian dialect, common Attic, Hellenistic or Biblical Greek. It was the common supra-regional form of Greek spoken and written during Hellenistic and Roman antiquity and the early Byzantine era, or Late Antiquity.

Mastaba:
: A rectangular structure with outward sloping sides.

Melqart:
: Known as the king of the city and was the tutelary Phoenician god of the city of Tyre. Also known as Baal.

Inv. No.
: Inventory number

nemes
: Striped head cloth worn by pharaohs in ancient Egypt.

ramleh:	A type of sandstone very common in the region of the Levant coast.
Safita:	A town in Tartus Governorate, north-western Syria, located to the southeast of Tartous and to the northwest of Krak des Chevaliers.
Salamis battle:	A battle fought between an Alliance of Greek city-states and the Persian Empire in the straits between the mainland and Salamis, an island in the Saronic Gulf near Athens.
Satraps:	The governors of the provinces of the ancient Median and Achaemenid (Persian) Empires and in several of their successors.

Bibliography

Akkermans, P. M. & Schwartz, G. M. (2003): *The Archaeology of Syria: From Complex Hunter-gatherers to Early Urban Societies (c. 16,000-300 BC)*. Cambridge: Cambridge University Press.

Elayi, J. & Haykal, M. (1996): *Nouvelles découvertes sur les usages funéraires des Phéniciens d'Arwad. Transeuphratène (suppl. 4)*. Paris: Gabalda.

Haykal, M. (1996a): *Amrīth and human occupation in Akar plain*. Damascus: Cooperative Society. (Arabic Edition).

Harden, D. (1963): *The Phoenicians: Ancient People and Places*. London: Thames and Hudson.

About the author

Bashar Mustafa, a citizen of Syria, received his formal education first at The University of Damascus, then at The University of Granada (Spain), from which he received his Ph.D. in Archaeology. A respected authority in his field, he is active in efforts to study and learn from our ancient past and to conserve the products of those ancient cultures for the benefit of all.

www.ingramcontent.com/pod-product-compliance
Lightning Source LLC
LaVergne TN
LVHW051704080426
835511LV00017B/2716